Fast Fusible Quilts

CROSS-STITCH QUILTS MADE EASY

TERRY MARTIN

Martingale™ & COMPANY

Credits

President Nancy J. Martin
CEO Daniel J. Martin
Publisher Jane Hamada
Editorial Director Mary V. Green
Editorial Project Manager Tina Cook
Technical Editor Darra Williamson
Copy Editor Ellen Balstad
Design and Production Manager Stan Green
Illustrator Laurel Strand
Cover Designer Stan Green
Text Designer Regina Girard
Photographer Brent Kane

That Patchwork Place®

That Patchwork Place® is an imprint of Martingale & Company™.

Martingale & Company
20205 144th Avenue NE
Woodinville, WA 98072-8478 USA
www.martingale-pub.com

Printed in China
06 05 04 03 02 01 8 7 6 5 4 3 2 1

Mission Statement

We are dedicated to providing quality products and service by working together to inspire creativity and to enrich the lives we touch.

Library of Congress Cataloging-in-Publication Data

Martin, Terry.

Fast fusible quilts : cross-stitch quilts made easy / Terry Martin.

p. cm.

ISBN 1-56477-367-1

1. Patchwork–Patterns. 2. Patchwork quilts. 3. Cross-stitch. I. Title.

TT835 .M27362 2001
746.46'041–dc21 2001032978

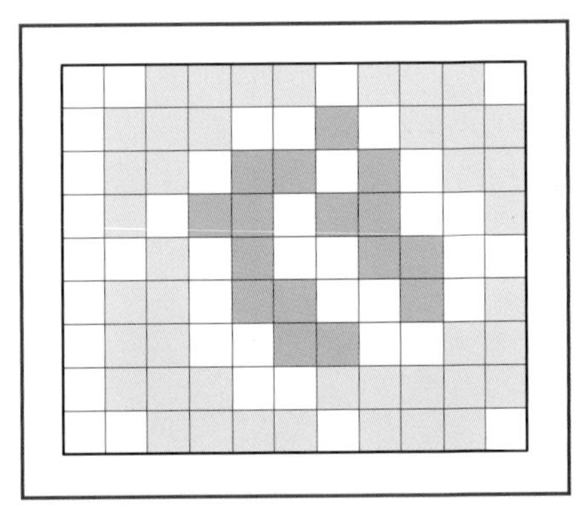

Dedication

To my husband, Ed, and daughter, McKenzie.
You are my joy, my life.

Acknowledgments

Many, many thanks go to:

Darra Williamson, my technical editor, for keeping me on the straight and narrow. This is the second book we have worked on together, and I couldn't think of doing this without you.

Barbara Dau, my quilter, who makes magic with her long-arm quilting machine. Her artist's flair brings out the best in a quilt top.

Mary Green and the folks at Martingale & Company, for hanging in there when the going got tough.

RJR Fashion Fabrics, for providing the beautiful cotton sateen fabric for my quilt ". . . And Pretty Flowers All in a Row."

And last, but certainly not least, to my friends and family, whom I couldn't live without.

CONTENTS

- ***Introduction ~ 6***
  - What Are Cross-Stitch Quilts? ~ 6
  - What Do You Mean, Interfacing a Quilt? ~ 6
  - Where Do You Get Your Inspiration? ~ 6
- ***Basic Techniques for Cross-Stitch Quilts ~ 7***
  - Working with Lightweight, Gridded, Fusible Interfacing ~ 7
  - Fabric Selection ~ 9
  - Sewing Equipment and Supplies ~ 10
  - Cutting the Fabric ~ 11
  - Design Layout ~ 12
  - Sewing the Seams ~ 13
  - Problem Solving ~ 14
  - A Word about Quilting ~ 16
- ***Adapting Your Favorite Charted Designs ~ 16***
  - Determining the Number of Squares ~ 16
  - Figuring Yardage ~ 17
  - Practicing the Technique ~ 17
- ***Projects***
  - Old Lace ~ 18
  - . . . And Pretty Flowers All in a Row ~ 22
  - The Monogram Quilt ~ 28
- ***Finishing Techniques ~ 40***
  - Adding Borders ~ 40
  - Preparing to Quilt ~ 40
  - Hand Quilting ~ 41
  - Machine Quilting ~ 42
  - Binding ~ 43
  - Adding a Sleeve ~ 44
  - Signing Your Quilt ~ 44
- ***Resources ~ 45***
- ***Bibliography ~ 45***
- ***Practice Motifs and Graph Paper ~ 46***
- ***About the Author ~ 48***

INTRODUCTION

What Are Cross-Stitch Quilts?

Postage-stamp quilts, made up of hundreds or thousands of small squares, have been popular with quiltmakers for a long time. Pioneer women frequently used every bit of fabric, even pieces as tiny as 1" square, to make these quilts for keeping their families warm at night. In the 1930s and 1940s, designer Anne Orr tried her own approach to the traditional technique of postage-stamp quilts. She converted her charted designs for cross-stitch into postage-stamp-style "cross-stitch" quilts and sold kits to reproduce them. Nowadays, you may look at these designs and think a computer created them because the small squares resemble the pixels in a digitized image. You may also think that it would be tedious to hand or machine stitch all of those small squares! As busy as we all are, it may even seem impossible to consider tackling one of these lovely—but time-consuming—projects. Take heart; you are about to discover a marvelously quick-and-easy solution for coping with the numerous pieces these designs require. With the help of fusible interfacing, you will be sitting in front of the television in no time, ironing board at lap level, laying out the design for your first project.

What Do You Mean, Interfacing a Quilt?

I thought you would never ask! I use lightweight, gridded, fusible interfacing to lay out and stitch my charted designs in fabric. I find this method easy and efficient, and I have created over a dozen cross-stitch quilts using this technique. Needless to say, I have discovered a lot of tricks and tips along the way! I plan to share them all with you on the following pages, which gives you the advantage of knowing them ahead of time and also where to find them quickly if you need them as you sew.

Where Do You Get Your Inspiration?

Throughout my life, I have dabbled in a variety of home crafts, and until the quilting bug bit me, my first passion was cross-stitch. I am a self-taught cross-stitcher, and when I first began, back in the late 1970s, I loved collecting designs and charts. However, at that time there were not a lot of cross-stitch patterns available. My searches for cross-stitch patterns often turned up old craft patterns for filet crochet, latch hook, and needlepoint instead. Consequently, I was forced to become resourceful. I soon realized that I could convert these same charted crochet, latch hook, and needlepoint patterns for use with cross-stitch. Often the vintage patterns were printed in black and white, and it was a good creativity exercise to add color to the designs with embroidery floss. It was about this time that I also discovered Dover Publications. Dover's inexpensive pamphlets, some of which feature charted designs taken from needlework dating back to the 1600s, were a real find. Granted, some of the designs looked dated and were not suitable for my tastes, but the geometric designs were timeless and I found myself extracting elements from large patterns to create my own look.

Fast Fusible Quilts, which has been a true joy to work on, represents the best of two worlds for me by encompassing my love of both cross-stitch and quilting. I've developed designs from a variety of inspirations and transformed one needlework art into another. An antique lace tablecloth, patterns on china, a needlepoint chair from my husband's side of the family, and a cross-stitch sampler made by my great-great-grandmother are just a few of the items that inspired the designs in this book. My best recommendation for inspiration is simply to look around you. I now see charted patterns everywhere, including in such odd things as a vintage bathroom throw rug I found in a secondhand and antiques store! The simple practice of looking keeps my creative "eyes" wide open—and very active!

Design inspiration can come from many sources.

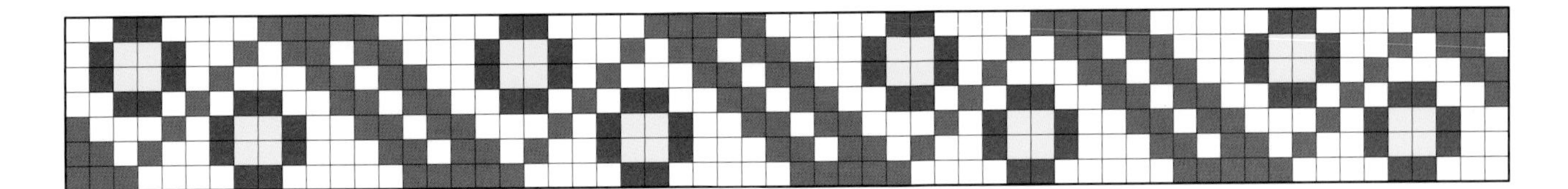

Basic Techniques for Cross-Stitch Quilts

Working with Lightweight, Gridded, Fusible Interfacing

Dina Pappas perfected the fusible interfacing process, which she calls the "fuse, fold, and stitch" method, in her book *Quick Watercolor Quilts* (That Patchwork Place, 1999). As soon as I read Dina's book and completed one of the projects, it struck me that it would be easy to adapt the process to convert cross-stitch and other similarly charted patterns into quilts.

Nonwoven, polyester, fusible interfacing is often used in garment sewing. In the lightweight gridded variety, which is what we will use for the projects in this book, a grid is printed on the non-fusible side with a light-colored ink. The grid squares vary in size; common sizes include 1", 1½", and 2". A variety of manufacturers make gridded, fusible interfacing; it is readily available in most fabric and well-stocked quilt shops.

I generally use a gridded, fusible interfacing with 1" squares because it comes on the bolt in convenient 44" to 48" widths, and it tends to be the grid-square size most commonly available. Read the manufacturer's instructions carefully before using any fusible product. Some suggest using a dry iron; others require steam. Products also differ in recommended pressing time.

Before you start a project, I highly recommend that you test the gridded, fusible interfacing by ironing it printed side up (fusible side down) to a piece of scrap fabric. It is possible that the ink from the printed grid will come off on your iron, which can in turn leave permanent black marks when you iron the top of your quilt! If you find that your fusible interfacing does this, simply make it a practice to iron your project from the front side only; avoid contact between your iron and the printed side of the fusible interfacing. That way, you're sure to avoid transferring the grid markings from the fusible interfacing to your iron, and ultimately to your quilt top. In fact, regardless of the test results, you may prefer to do as I do and always iron from the front side. It's better to be safe than sorry!

When you are ready to start pressing, be sure to press carefully to avoid distorting the fabric pieces. Use an up-and-down motion, rather than sliding the iron back and forth.

If, despite your best efforts, you manage to transfer markings from the fusible interfacing to your iron, refer to the manufacturer's instructions for cleaning the iron's surface. As an alternative, you may want to try the method I use: allow your iron to produce a good dose of steam; then, wearing an oven mitt, wipe the surface clean with a piece of white muslin.

Another factor you'll want to consider as you work is the orientation of the fusible interfacing. Similar to woven fabrics, these fusible interfacings are stretchier across their width. Since you will press seams constantly when constructing the charted design portion of the quilts, which I will refer to as pieced panels, the orientation can become important. The repeated stress of pressing interfacing that stretches one way more than the other can result in a distorted pieced panel. If that happens, you can often make adjustments to the quilt top by trimming the pieced panel, altering the border measurements, or creating a slightly different-sized quilt than indicated by the instructions. But of course it's best to eliminate, or at least minimize, this situation from the start!

Orientation also becomes a factor when the project requires more than one pieced panel of interfacing, such as in "The Monogram Quilt" on page 28. (If you are going to be distorted, you might as well be distorted in the same direction!) Whenever possible, I try to keep the interfacing running *lengthwise* across my design. I generally find this to be the most efficient use of the interfacing, given its width.

If you have difficulty determining the lengthwise and crosswise orientation by sight alone, try this simple test. Grasp an 18"-wide piece of fusible interfacing between your hands and pull gently. Rotate the interfacing one turn (90°) and pull gently again. The difference will be obvious: one side will have more stretch or give than the other.

Once you determine which side is lengthwise (the side with less give), label it with an erasable fabric marker or insert a straight pin along one lengthwise edge. You'll be able to use this mark to identify the lengthwise side immediately until you stitch the fabric squares in place.

Pulling gently reveals considerable stretch across the width of the interfacing.

There is much less "give" when the interfacing is turned 90°, along the length.

All of the designs in this book call for fabric squares that are cut 1½" x 1½", to finish 1" square when sewn. It is not necessary, however, that the grid-square sizes on the fusible interfacing match the size of either the cut or stitched squares; you may use any size of grid squares for your project. You are merely using the vertical and horizontal markings on the interfacing as a guide for keeping the squares in neat, straight rows. For example, I use interfacing with 1" grid squares, but my designs start with 1½" cut squares of fabric. Even though the sizes of the squares don't match, I know that every two squares of fabric will line up to a vertical or horizontal line on the interfacing. See how this is demonstrated in the illustration below.

1" x 1" gridded interfacing (fusible side up)

1½" x 1½" unfinished squares of fabric

Fabric Selection

As a quilter, I always use 100 percent–cotton fabric, which is durable and handles well. However, the use of fusible interfacing to create cross-stitch style quilts provides the perfect opportunity to try different types of fabrics. Normally tricky-to-handle silk, rayon, and viscose fabrics become much more user-friendly. Since you are securing the cut squares to interfacing, you eliminate the concern of these pieces raveling or distorting. So although I chose to use 100 percent–cotton fabrics for the projects in this book and include yardage requirements that are based on 42" of usable fabric after preshrinking, I encourage you to experiment with not-so-typical quilt fabrics. Do keep in mind, however, that whatever fabric you choose, it will be pressed continually throughout the construction process, most likely using steam.

I identify the fabrics used for the pieced panels as falling into one of two main categories: design fabric and background fabric. Any other part of the quilt top, such as the sashings and borders, are considered separately.

Background Fabric

Background fabric provides a backdrop for the design motifs and acts as a visual resting place between the various elements. Some quilts, such as "The Monogram Quilt" on page 28, include a variety of background fabrics. The seven fabrics in the Plaid blocks surrounding the monogram, and the blue-print fabric outside the monogram oval, are all considered background fabric.

While selecting background fabric, consider how it will frame the design. I prefer solid fabrics, or those with a small-scale, tone-on-tone print. You'll find a huge selection of these rich tone-on-tone prints being manufactured today, in every colorway imaginable. I find they can add movement and depth to the key design without overpowering it.

Background fabric

Design Fabric

Just as the name implies, the design fabrics establish the key motifs of the charted pattern. In "The Monogram Quilt" mentioned earlier and pictured on page 28, the monogram, the small flowers floating around the monogram, and the dark green oval are considered the design fabrics.

Design fabric should stand apart from the background fabric and "read" well. I generally recommend choosing bold, richly-colored fabrics that are solid or have a small overall print. Remember: these squares finish 1" square, which doesn't allow a lot of area for the print to show.

Of course, you can make exceptions as I did in "Old Lace" on page 18. In this quilt, the design fabric, which I also used for the border, is a rather large print. I intentionally chose this fabric because I wanted a lacy, open look to the design. This fabric also introduced a touch of green into the color palette, enriching the overall look of this two-fabric quilt.

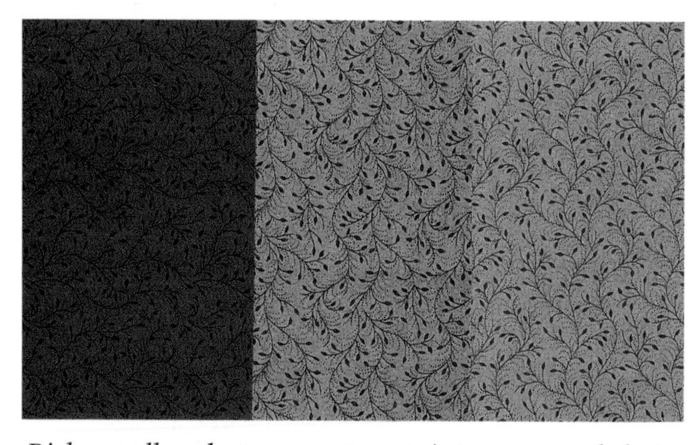

Rich, small-scale, tone-on-tone prints are a good choice for design fabric. These fabrics "read" well in the overall design.

These fern prints, with their mottled backgrounds, provide subtle—but rich—textures.

Audition your fabrics by cutting a few 1" squares of both your design and background selections. This will give you a preview of how they'll work together in the finished quilt.

Sewing Equipment and Supplies

Sewing machine: To machine piece, you'll need a sewing machine that has a good straight stitch. You'll also need a walking foot or darning foot for machine quilting. Take a moment to clean and oil your machine. In fact, get into the practice of cleaning your machine before every project. Cotton is a great fiber, but it creates lint under the feed dogs that can interfere with the smooth running of your sewing machine.

Rotary-cutting tools: You will need a rotary cutter, cutting mat, and clear acrylic ruler. The 6" x 24" ruler works well for cutting the long strips you'll need for these projects. You'll also appreciate a small square ruler, such as the 6" x 6" size, for lining up the first cut in each fabric and for crosscutting the fabric strips into individual squares.

Thread: Use a good-quality, all-purpose cotton or cotton-covered-polyester thread. Choose a neutral color thread, such as gray, that won't show through when you are piecing light and dark fabrics together.

Needles: For machine piecing most fabrics, a size 10/70 or 12/80 needle works well.

Pins: Long, fine "quilters' pins" with glass or plastic heads are easy to see and useful for pinning multiple layers.

Scissors: Use your best scissors to cut fabric only. Small, 4" scissors with sharp points are handy for clipping thread.

Seam ripper: Use this tool to remove stitches from incorrectly sewn seams. The smaller and finer the seam ripper the better, since your machine stitches may be close together—especially at seamed intersections.

Marking tools: Use a sharp No. 2 pencil or fine-lead mechanical pencil on lighter-colored fabrics, and a silver or yellow marking pencil on darker fabrics. Chalk pencils or chalk-wheel markers also make clear marks on fabric. Be sure to test your marking tool to make sure you can remove the marks easily.

Iron and ironing board: A small craft iron set up near your sewing machine gives you quick access for pressing as you stitch. Use a standard steam iron for pressing rows and larger sections of the quilt.

Fusible interfacing: Lightweight, gridded, fusible interfacing is available from a variety of suppliers, including your local quilt shop or fabric store. (Also see "Resources" on page 45.) Preprinted grids feature squares that range from 1" to 1½" to 2". Refer to "Working with Lightweight, Gridded, Fusible Interfacing" on pages 7–9 for guidance in using these handy grids for accurate patchwork.

Cutting the Fabric

All cutting measurements given in the project instructions are for rotary cutting and include standard ¼"-wide seam allowances. For those unfamiliar with rotary cutting, a brief introduction is provided here.

1. Fold the fabric and match selvages, aligning the crosswise and lengthwise grains as much as possible. Place the folded edge closest to you on the cutting mat. Align a square ruler along the folded edge of the fabric. Then place a long, straight ruler to the left of the square ruler, just covering the uneven raw edges of the left side of the fabric.

   Remove the square ruler and cut along the right edge of the long ruler, rolling the rotary cutter away from you. Discard this strip. (Reverse this procedure if you are left-handed.)

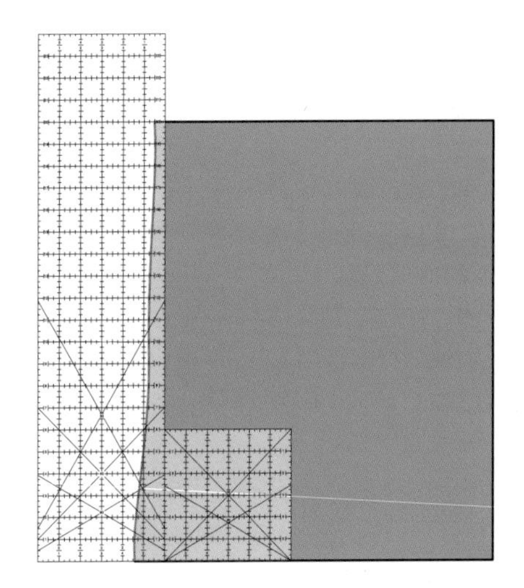

2. To cut strips, align the required measurement on the ruler with the newly cut edge of the fabric. For example, to cut a 1½"-wide strip, place the 1½" ruler mark on the edge of the fabric.

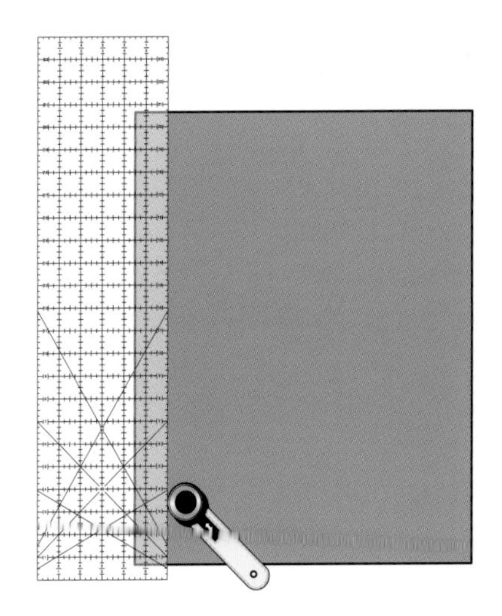

3. To cut squares, cut strips in the required widths. Trim away the selvage ends of the strip. Align the required measurement on the ruler with the left edge of the strip and cut a square. Continue cutting squares until you have the number needed.

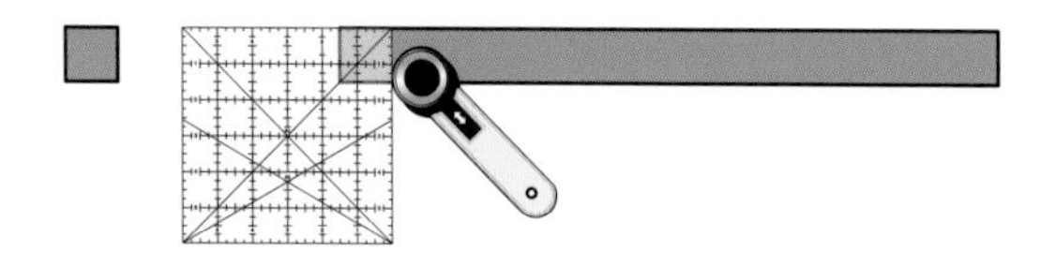

All of the projects in this book begin with 1½"-wide strips, cut on the crosswise grain of fabric from selvage to selvage. These strips are crosscut into the 1½" (unfinished) squares that are used to make the quilt design and fill in the background areas.

I've included a cutting chart for each project that tells you how many strips and squares of each color you'll need to cut for that specific design. I've also provided a design chart for each project, with each square equaling one square of fabric. Note that each project design chart includes large areas—usually as part of the background—that are all one color. Sometimes you can partially fill these areas with strips (or with combinations of strips and squares), rather than entirely with individual squares. Using strips makes both the cutting and piecing process even less time-consuming. Once you sew the seams, no one will ever know that you didn't cut each square individually. The choice is up to you.

If you do decide to fill areas in your quilt with a combination of strips and squares, here's a quick overview of how the process works. If I note a large, single-colored area in my design chart (such as the subtle blue-print background in "The Monogram Quilt" on page 28), I plan ahead when cutting the fabric strips. Instead of crosscutting the strips into 1½" squares, I leave several full-length strips, and cut the remaining full-length strips into lengths equal to the lengths of two (1½" x 3"), four (1½" x 6"), and six (1½" x 9") unfinished squares. As I lay out the design on the gridded interfacing, I can pick and choose the segments to fit. I can also cut individual squares as I need them. Refer to the illustration below, noting how it demonstrates this layout process.

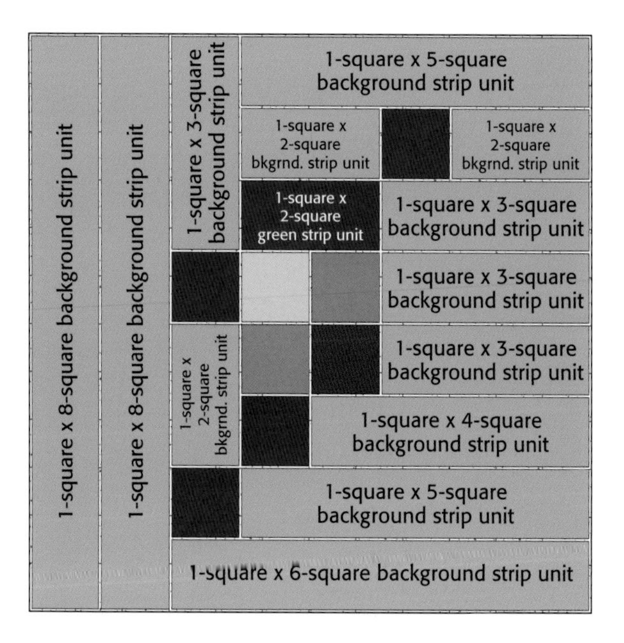

Design Layout

Once you cut all of your fabric into strips and squares and cut a piece of gridded, fusible interfacing as indicated in the individual project instructions, the fun begins! I find it most comfortable and efficient to work while sitting at my ironing board, with my fabric strips, squares, and design chart on a little table beside me. My ironing board is covered with inexpensive muslin, which helps me see the grid on the interfacing much more clearly and protects the ironing-board cover from any interfacing residue.

To lay out the design, smooth the gridded interfacing, fusible side up, on your pressing surface. Let the excess interfacing drape over the ironing board's back edge. Beginning in the lower-right-hand corner of the interfacing, place the squares (and strips if you are using them) right side up, carefully following the design chart provided in the individual project instructions. Use the grid's horizontal and vertical lines to keep the squares and strips straight and even.

When laying out the first or last row of squares, and the first and last square in each row, it's not essential that the entire square be on the fusible interfacing. So long as a portion of the square overlaps the fusible interfacing, you'll be fine. Just be sure to use the vertical and horizontal markings on the grid to help keep your rows straight, as usual.

Lay out an area approximately 12" square (8 squares x 8 squares); then stop to press the fabric squares to the fusible interfacing, following the manufacturer's instructions. This step secures the squares as you shift the interfacing across your pressing surface. Do not slide the iron across the design surface or you risk shifting the squares out of place. Instead, lift and reposition the iron with an up-and-down motion, placing it carefully so that it doesn't touch the exposed fusible. If this does happen, clean the residue from your iron's soleplate immediately.

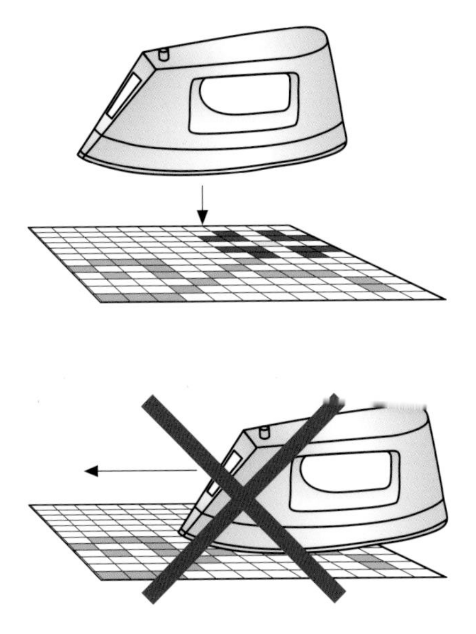

Continue positioning the iron and pressing small sections until you have fused the entire pieced panel.

If the iron temperature is not set correctly, or if you press too lightly or for too short a time, the fabric squares may not fuse securely to the interfacing, which can be good *and* bad. An initial light fusing gives you the opportunity to remove and reposition misplaced squares and strips without tearing the interfacing. On the other hand, if you wait several days before sewing, squares may float away en route to the sewing machine! If it will be awhile before you are able to proceed with your project, take the time to re-press the pieced panel before you sew to ensure a good bond between the interfacing and the fabric.

After you have fused the entire design to the interfacing, take a moment to inspect it carefully. Place it on the floor or a design wall so you can step back and view the whole design. This is the best time to catch layout mistakes—before the seams are sewn! If you do find a mistake, gently remove the piece, taking care not to tear the interfacing, and replace it with a newly cut fabric piece.

Sewing the Seams

Starting at the right edge, fold the first two vertical rows right sides together and finger press. Stitch the seam from top to bottom, taking a scant ¼"-wide seam allowance. Since you are stitching four layers (two each of fabric and interfacing), the bulky seam takes up more than the usual amount of fabric. By sewing just short of the usual ¼"-wide seam allowance, you allow for this bulk and ensure a more accurate 1" finished square. If you do not sew a scant ¼"-wide seam, the individual squares will not be the desired finished size and the size of everything else in the quilt will be affected, including sashing and borders. Measurements for all components of each quilt are based on pieced panels that finish accurately to the desired size plus ¼" on each edge for seam allowances.

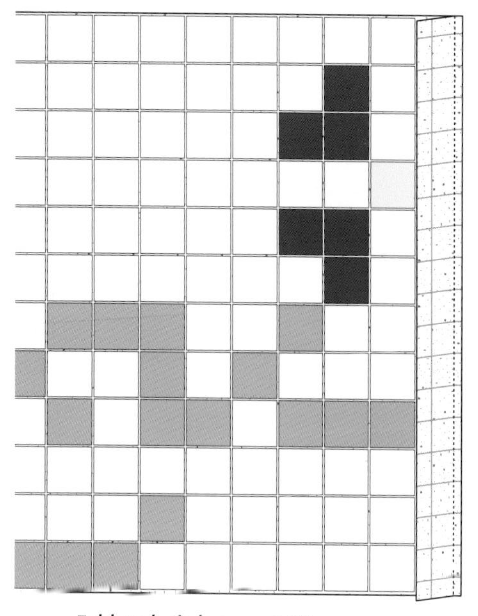

Fold and stitch a scant ¼" seam.

After you sew approximately six vertical rows, stop and press the seams to one side, pressing from the front side of the pieced panel. Pressing the rows prevents the pieced panel from getting caught in the stitching as you sew successive seams, especially since the stitched rows have a tendency to curl in on themselves. As you press, gently tug on the pieced panel to open the seams as much as possible; this will help you distribute the bulk and maintain a finished 1" square. Repeat until you have stitched each vertical row.

Clip the seams at the square intersections to further distribute the bulk, and finger-press seam allowances in opposite directions from row to row. I know that clipping seams can be scary, but take heart: if you inadvertently clip through a seam, that clipped seam will be concealed by the seam allowance when you stitch the horizontal seam.

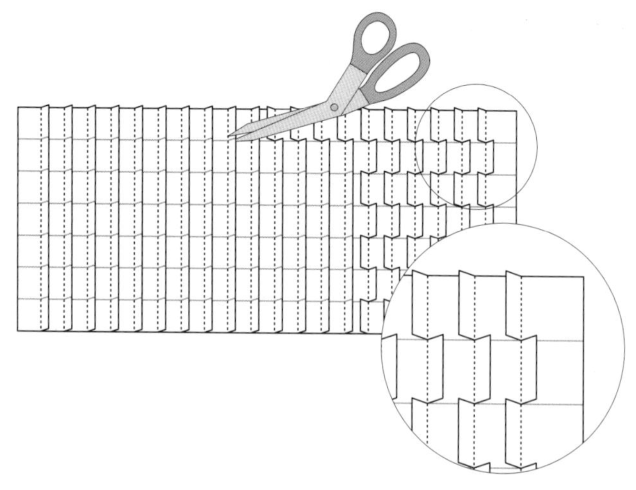

In the same manner used for the vertical rows, stitch and press each horizontal row. Square up the finished panel by pressing it from the front side, using lots of steam. Follow the individual project instructions to complete the quilt top.

Problem Solving

I encountered a few odd situations while making these quilts that I would like to share with you. Perhaps my experiences will help you out if you find yourself similarly challenged!

One of my problems came after I had just completed a quilt top and was about to prepare the quilt "sandwich" for basting. I discovered a couple of squares out of place in the design. I was stumped as to how to fix this, since the seams were sewn already. I ended up trying two different remedies. The first remedy was to "unsew" the seams around each misplaced square and replace it with a square of the correct fabric, which did *not* work very well! I had a difficult time unpicking the seams with my seam ripper, and by this stage in the process, the fabric was so firmly pressed to the interfacing that the interfacing tore. Once the squares were replaced and seams resewn, the squares were distorted. My second—and best—remedy was to simply appliqué the appropriate fabric over the misplaced squares. By the time the quilt was quilted, no one could find the error!

Another challenge I faced involved separate blocks or panels that needed to match but were off by an inch or more! I had asked several coworkers to make blocks for a friendship quilt and, as is often the case, every block came back a different size. I had no choice but to trim some blocks and add to others, but I was worried that my alterations would be obvious, especially since I was working with blocks based on same-sized squares. But surprisingly, these changes weren't obvious at all! By the time the quilt top was quilted, the motif on each block shone through and it was not at all apparent that some squares in the blocks weren't quite square.

Careful alterations solved the problem of different-sized blocks in this friendship quilt.

If the size of your fabric squares is different from the size of the squares on the gridded, fusible interfacing, you will notice that some seams will not be folded on a printed line on the interfacing. For example, if you use 1" gridded, fusible interfacing with 1½" fabric squares, some of the folds will be midway between the printed lines—exactly ½" between the printed lines on the interfacing. If you use a ¼" stitching foot, you will notice that the foot fits perfectly between the edge of the fold and the printed line. The ¼" stitching foot will keep you on track for sewing an accurate seam. Remember to sew a scant ¼" seam by shifting the project slightly to the left before stitching. I like to see a small bit of white space between the left outside edge of the ¼" foot and the line printed on the gridded interfacing. See the following illustration for an example.

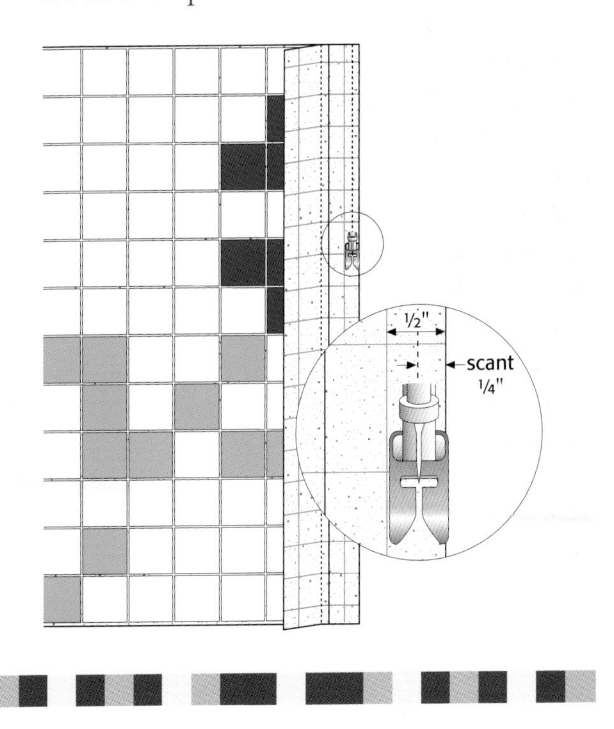

A Word about Quilting

Because of the extra layer added by the fusible interfacing and the many seams involved, I strongly recommend machine quilting at least the pieced panels of these quilts. You may choose to do as I have done, and machine quilt throughout. However, if you enjoy hand quilting, you can easily combine the two techniques by hand quilting in the borders that are not pieced.

Once you determine the quilting method you will use, select the areas that you will quilt and how you will quilt them. One option is to quilt all or part of the pieced panel in the ditch. If you wish, you can use colorful rayon or metallic thread to add extra texture and sparkle. (See "Old Lace" on page 18). Or, you may prefer to quilt the background area of the panel with a meandering, stippled, or other overall pattern. If the areas covered by the design motifs are small or scattered enough, you can choose not to quilt them. Not quilting these areas really causes them to stand out, almost as though they have been trapuntoed! (See "...And Pretty Flowers All in a Row" on page 22 and "The Monogram Quilt" on page 28).

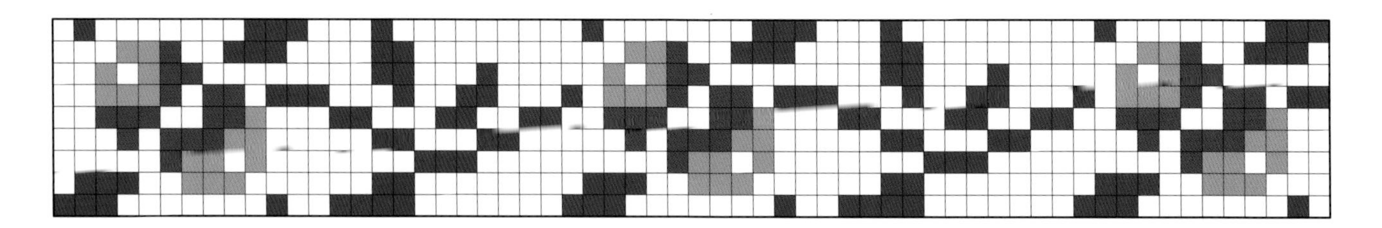

ADAPTING
YOUR FAVORITE CHARTED DESIGNS

It is very easy to translate your favorite charted designs to beautiful quilts. Keep in mind the designs should be simple and easy to "read," without a lot of color changes. If you work from a chart that is in black and white, you will need to color it in to determine the fabric quantities.

Determining the Number of Squares

1. To calculate the total number of squares in your design, count the number of vertical and horizontal squares and multiply these two numbers together. For example, if the entire charted design is 23 squares wide and 15 squares high, the total number of squares for the design will be 345 squares (23 x 15 = 345).
2. Count and list the number of squares of each color needed for the various design motifs.
3. Determine the required number of background squares by subtracting the total number of design-motif squares (step 2) from the total number of squares in the charted design (step 1). For example, if your charted design totals 345 squares and includes 75 red squares, 42 green squares, and 97 yellow squares, you'll need 101 background squares (345 – 214 [75 + 42 + 97] = 101).

Note: If you choose to make "The Monogram Quilt" on page 28, you'll need this information and the following information on figuring yardage to determine the number of background squares and the yardage required to complete your personal monogram design.

Figuring Yardage

You can figure the yardage you'll need for each fabric in your charted design based on the finished size of the squares you plan to use. For squares that finish 1" x 1", as is the case for all of the projects in this book, you'll need to cut 1½" x 1½" pieces. A 1½"-wide strip cut from a 42"-wide fabric will yield twenty-eight 1½" squares. To determine how many strips you'll need of a specific fabric, divide the number of squares required from that fabric by 28 and round up to the next whole number. Multiply the number of strips required by the unfinished (cut) size of the squares; in this case, 1½". Round up to the next ⅛ or ¼ yard, and you'll know how much yardage you'll need to cut the necessary squares.

As an example, let's say your design requires seventy-five 1" squares of red fabric, which means the unfinished or cut size of each square will be 1½". The math would work as follows: 75 ÷ 28 = 2.67 (or 3 strips); 3 strips x 1½" = 6" (rounded up to ¼ yard) of fabric.

To determine the piece size of the gridded, fusible interfacing that you'll need, multiply both the number of vertical squares and the number of horizontal squares in the charted design by the unfinished (cut) measurement of the individual squares. For example, a charted design that includes 1" finished (1½" cut) squares and measures 23 squares across by 15 squares high would require a 34½" x 22½" piece of fusible interfacing, since 23 x 1½" = 34½" and 15 x 1½" = 22½".

Practicing the Technique

I am really blessed to have a cross-stitch sampler made by my great-great-grandmother. She was eleven years old when she made it in the mid-1840s, and the colors are still brilliant (see photo of the sampler at right). On page 46, I have reproduced a few of the motifs from this sampler, including a traditional-looking cross-stitch bird, a beautiful heart, a crown, a topiary, and a few border designs. Now that you have all of the tools and information needed to create a cross-stitch quilt, I encourage you to practice with some of these motifs to design and make your own quilt. The motifs are shown in the colors that appear on the original sampler. I purposely did not include the square counts of the motifs, fabric requirements, or size of the gridded, fusible interfacing so that you can practice calculating and creating on your own. I have also provided blank graph paper on page 47 that you can photocopy and use to design your own cross-stitch quilts.

Cross-stitch sampler made by my great-great-grandmother

Old Lace

Old Lace by Terry Martin, 2001, Snohomish, Washington, 43" x 43".

I found a simple black-and-white design for the center motif and bordered it with the same fabric to create a simple but stunning two-fabric quilt.

I found this particular design in *101 Folk Art Designs for Counted Cross-Stitch and Other Needlecrafts*, edited by Carter Houck (see "Bibliography" on page 45). It reminds me of a bit of lace I might find in my grandmother's lace basket. She kept a covered wicker sewing basket full of lace that she collected over the years or salvaged from an old dress or table scarf. I have the basket now and cherish it deeply.

This is an easy-and-fun project to get you started using gridded, fusible interfacing. It requires only two fabrics, is simple enough for a beginner, and makes a stunning quilt for a wall or tabletop. Audition your fabrics carefully to achieve a good contrast between background and design. For this quilt, I was trying to achieve an open, delicate, lacy look, so I chose a large-scale print for the design. Note that it's not a choice I would normally make, or one I would recommend for the other projects in this book (see "Fabric Selection" on page 9), but it worked out nicely in this instance. I also found the perfect partner in the background fabric. The warm color and the richness of the mottled print enhance the overall look without detracting from the lacy design.

Quilt Size: 43" x 43"

Materials

42"-wide fabric; 44"-wide (minimum), gridded, fusible interfacing

1⅓ yds. lightweight, gridded, fusible interfacing

1⅜ yds. print for design and border

1 yd. contrasting tone-on-tone or mottled print for background

2⅝ yds. fabric for backing

½ yd. fabric for binding*

**I used the same print that I used for the design and border.*

Cutting for the Pieced Panel

This quilt is based on 1" finished squares. Cut all strips 1½" x 42", which includes ¼"-wide seam allowances.

Fabric	Total Number of Strips	Total Number of Squares
Design fabric	13	353
Background fabric	22	608

Cutting Borders and Binding

From the remaining print (design) fabric, cut:

4 strips, each 6½" x 42", for borders

From the binding fabric, cut:

5 strips, each 2½" x 42"

Layout and Construction of the Pieced Panel

Note: *Refer to "Basic Techniques for Cross-Stitch Quilts" on pages 7–16 for guidance as needed.*

1. Cut a 46½" square from the 1⅓ yards of gridded, fusible interfacing. If your interfacing is not wide enough to cut a square this large, cut a piece that measures 46½" by the width of the interfacing (minimum of 44" wide).
2. Spread the gridded interfacing, fusible side up, on your ironing surface. Run the lengthwise edges horizontally.
3. Begin in the lower-right-hand corner of the fusible interfacing. Position the squares (and strips if you are using them) as shown in the design chart on page 21, carefully aligning the pieces with the vertical and horizontal lines on the grid. Stop periodically to press the pieces to the fusible interfacing as you go, following the manufacturer's instructions regarding iron temperature, use of steam, and so on.

If your piece of fusible interfacing measures slightly smaller than 46½" from top to bottom, it may still be possible to fit all of the squares on this single piece. Refer to the tip box on page 13 for guidance.

If you are unable to fit the top row of squares on the large piece of fusible interfacing, cut an additional 1½" x 46½" strip of interfacing. Lay out and fuse the top row of 1½" squares to this strip. The strip may then be pieced to the top edge of the larger unit.

4. When the entire panel has been laid out and fused, stitch the vertical and horizontal seams as described in "Sewing the Seams" on pages 13–14. Finish by steam pressing the entire panel.

Adding Borders

Refer to "Adding Borders" on page 40 for guidance as needed with measuring, trimming, and sewing the 6½" x 42" border strips to your quilt. Add border strips to the top and bottom first; then add the border strips to the sides of the quilt. Press the seams toward the borders.

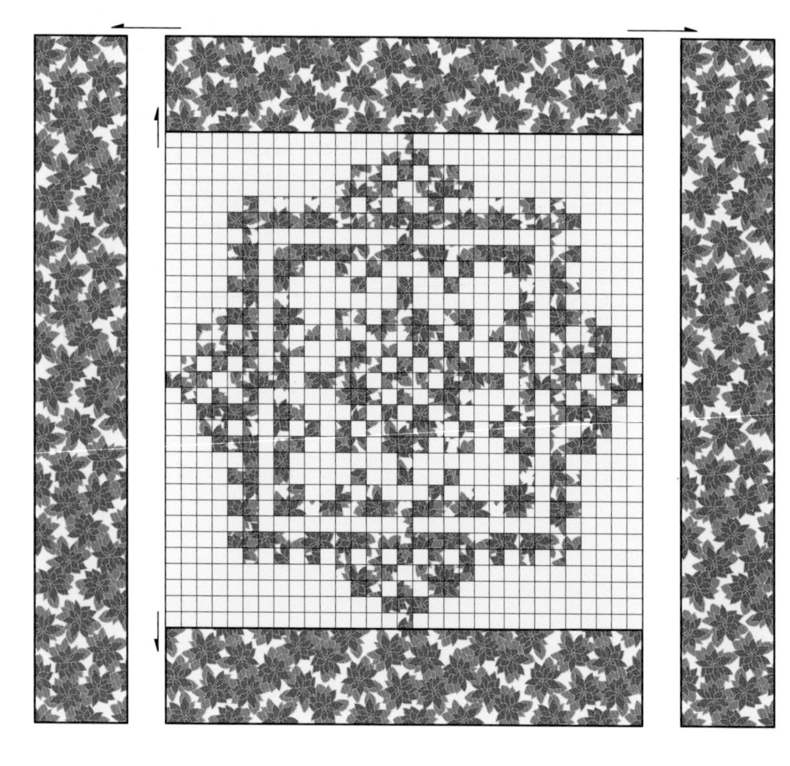

Finishing

Refer to "Finishing Techniques" on pages 40–44 for guidance as needed with marking, basting, quilting, and finishing your quilt.

1. Divide the backing fabric crosswise into 2 equal panels of approximately 47" each. Remove the selvages and join the pieces to make a single, large backing panel.
2. Center and layer the quilt top and the batting over the backing; baste.
3. Quilt as desired.
4. Trim the batting and backing even with the edges of the quilt top.
5. Use the 2½" x 42" strips to make the binding. Sew the binding to the quilt, adding a hanging sleeve if desired.
6. Make a label and attach it to your quilt.

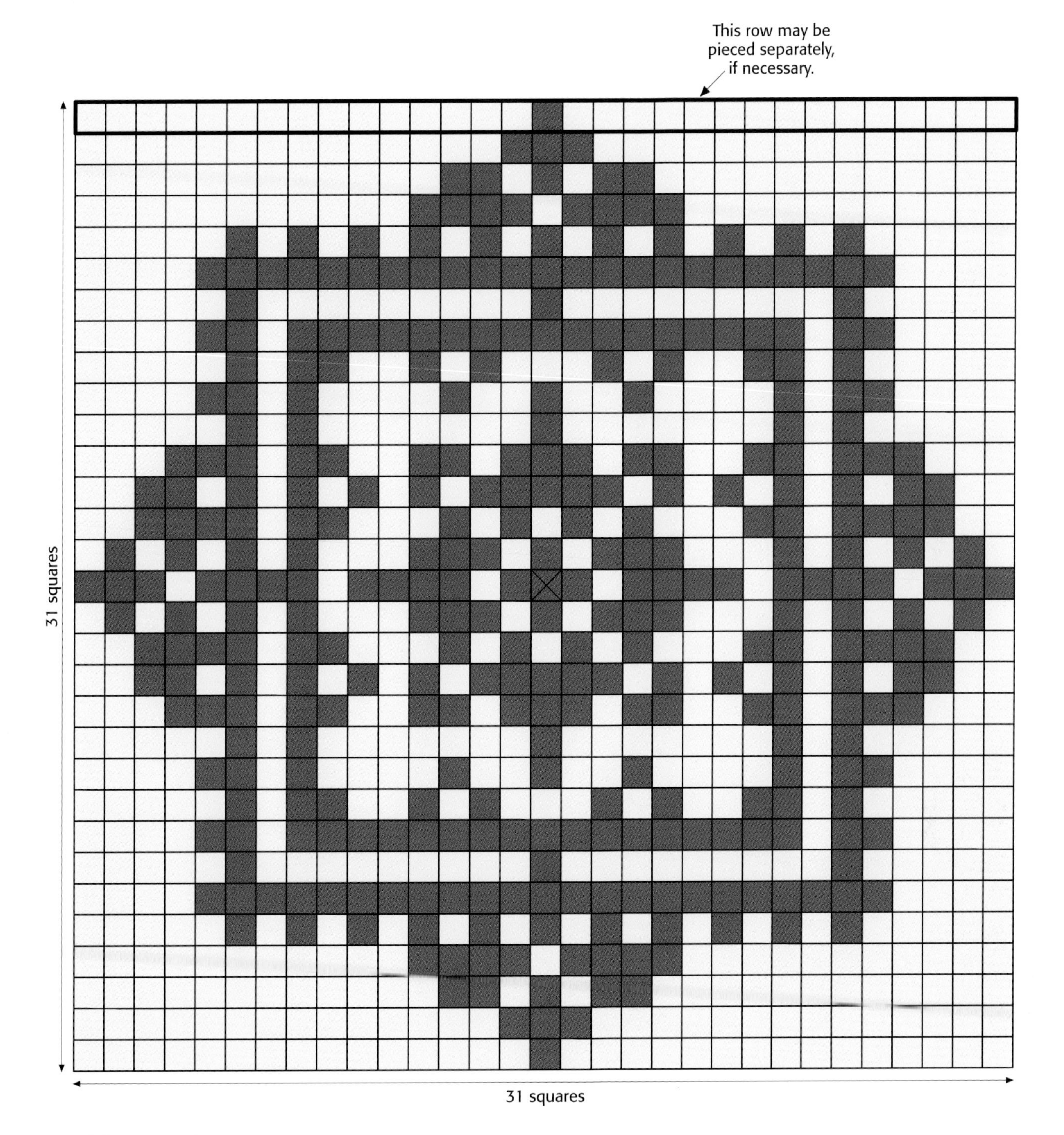
This row may be pieced separately, if necessary.
31 squares
31 squares
Center of design

. . . And Pretty Flowers All in a Row

. . . *And Pretty Flowers All in a Row* by Terry Martin, 2000, Snohomish, Washington, 89" x 103". Quilted by Barbara Dau.

My fascination with bar or row quilts led me to create this beautiful floral quilt using sumptuous, 100 percent–cotton sateen fabric.

I had the good fortune to work with various fabric manufacturers while designing the projects for this book, and I instantly fell in love with the beautiful colors of RJR Fashion Fabrics' 100 percent–cotton sateens. (Yes, sateen!) With their rich luster and smooth, silky feel, I knew these fabrics were the perfect choice for a bed-sized quilt for our master bedroom. The colors are varied and sophisticated, and I sensed that it would be easy and lots of fun to decorate a bedroom around them.

I love bar quilts and enjoy designing them by using fusible interfacing and old cross-stitch charts (see "Adapting Your Favorite Charted Designs" on pages 16–17). These panel designs were created by Anne Orr; I found them in a variety of different sources.

Even though this quilt features a floral motif, it's not too feminine. The panels are constructed separately, so the quilt comes together quickly, and the large, lush, dark teal border makes the perfect canvas for both the hand and machine quilter.

This is a great quilt for using up leftovers and small bits of fabric. After reviewing the number of squares required for each panel, you may discover that you have all the fabric you need right in your scrap bag. You can make the quilt even scrappier by using different background fabric for each of the panels.

Quilt Size: 89" x 103"

Materials

42"-wide fabrics; 44"-wide, gridded, fusible interfacing

7½ yds. lightweight, gridded, fusible interfacing

⅛ yd. *each* of yellow, dark lavender, lavender, pink, mustard, dark mauve, and blue solid for designs

¼ yd. *each* of red, medium rose, dark rose, navy blue, dark blue, green #2, pale pink, tan, and orange solid for designs

1 yd. green #1 solid for designs (panels 1, 4, 5, 6, and 7)

4¾ yds. cream solid for background and sashing

3¼ yds. dark teal solid for border

8 yds. fabric for backing

¾ yd. fabric for binding*

**I used a mix of sateens left over from the quilt.*

Cutting for the Pieced Panels

This quilt is based on 1" finished squares. Unless instructed otherwise, cut all fabric strips 1½" x 42", which includes ¼"-wide seam allowances.

Panel 1

Fabric	Total Number of Strips	Total Number of Squares
Yellow	2	32
Red	3	64
Green #1	5	125
Cream (background)	8	199
One 10½" x 90" strip of gridded, fusible interfacing		

Panel 2

Fabric	Total Number of Strips	Total Number of Squares
Medium rose	3	57
Dark rose	3	63
Navy blue	4	90
Cream (background)	12	330
One 13½" x 90" strip of gridded, fusible interfacing		

Panel 3

Fabric	Total Number of Strips	Total Number of Squares
Dark blue	3	60
Yellow	1 (1½" x 7½")	5
Green #2	4	100
Cream (background)	18	495
One 16½" x 90" strip of gridded, fusible interfacing		

Panel 4

Fabric	Total Number of Strips	Total Number of Squares
Dark lavender	2	48
Lavender	2	48
Green #1	4	108
Cream (background)	13	336
One 13½" x 90" strip of gridded, fusible interfacing		

Panel 5

Fabric	Total Number of Strips	Total Number of Squares
Pink	2	48
Pale pink	5	126
Green #1	3	80
Cream (background)	11	286
One 13½" x 90" strip of gridded, fusible interfacing		

Panel 6

Fabric	Total Number of Strips	Total Number of Squares
Mustard	2	48
Dark mauve	2	51
Green #1	2	30
Tan	3	66
Cream (background)	9	225
One 10½" x 90" strip of gridded, fusible interfacing		

Panel 7

Fabric	Total Number of Strips	Total Number of Squares
Blue	1	28
Orange	4	87
Green #1	4	112
Cream (background)	7	193
One 10½" x 90" strip of gridded fusible interfacing		

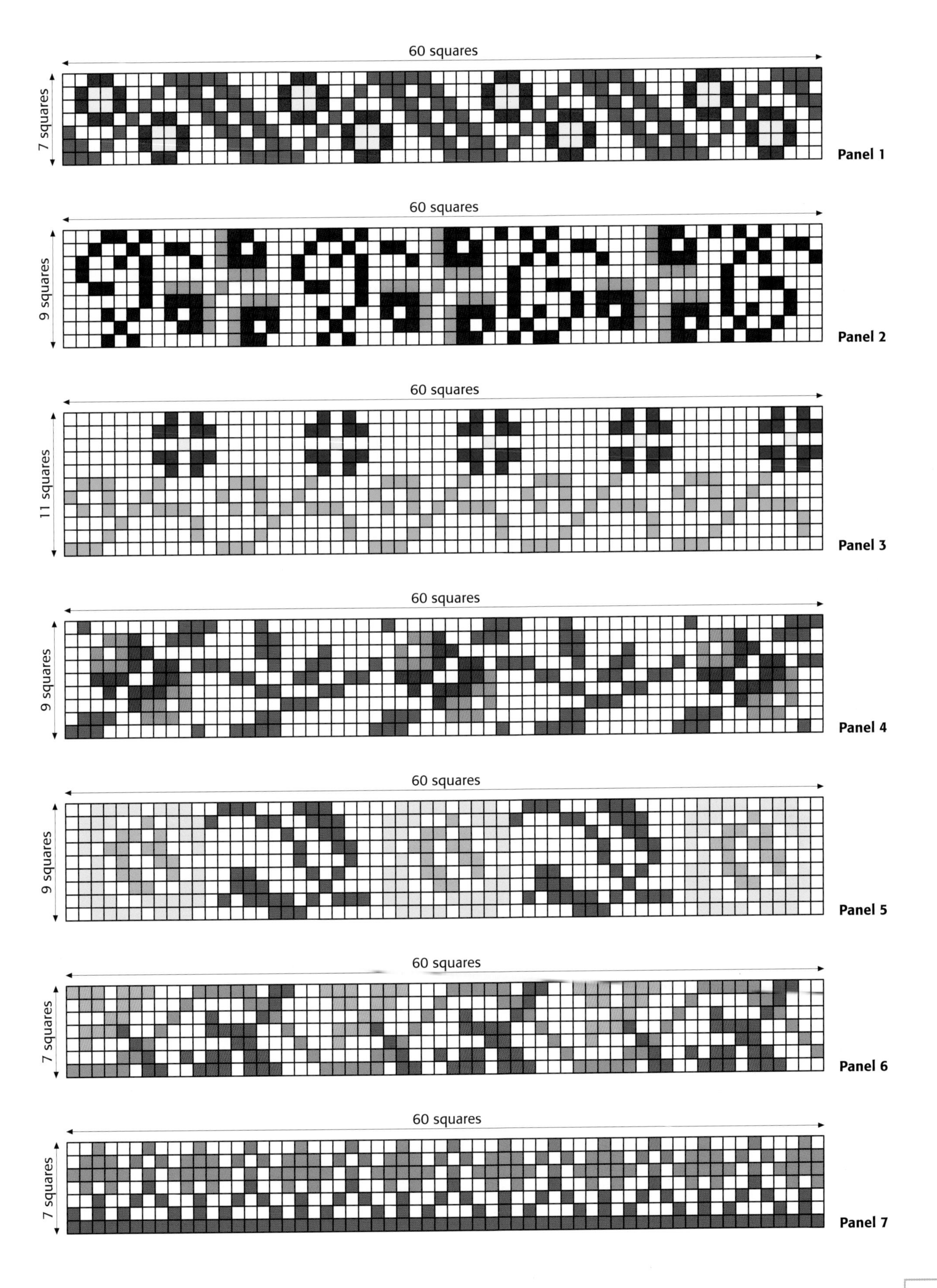
60 squares
7 squares
Panel 1
60 squares
9 squares
Panel 2
60 squares
11 squares
Panel 3
60 squares
9 squares
Panel 4
60 squares
9 squares
Panel 5
60 squares
7 squares
Panel 6
60 squares
7 squares
Panel 7

Cutting Sashing, Borders, and Binding

From the remaining cream solid, cut:
16 strips, each 3" x 42", for sashing

From the dark teal solid, cut
9 strips, each 12½" x 42", for borders

From the binding fabric, cut:
10 strips, each 2½" x 42"

Layout and Construction of the Pieced Panels

Note: Refer to "Basic Techniques for Cross-Stitch Quilts" on pages 7–16 for guidance as needed. There are 7 pieced panels in this quilt. Each panel is constructed separately. Follow the instructions below to make each panel.

1. Spread the appropriately sized strip of gridded interfacing, fusible side up, on your ironing surface. Run the lengthwise edges horizontally.
2. Begin in the lower-right-hand corner of the grid. Position the squares (and strips if you are using them) as shown in the design chart on page 25. Carefully align the pieces with the vertical and horizontal lines on the grid. Stop periodically to press the pieces to the fusible interfacing as you go, following the manufacturer's instructions regarding iron temperature, use of steam, and so on.
3. When the entire panel has been laid out and fused, stitch the vertical and horizontal seams as described in "Sewing the Seams" on pages 13–14. Finish by steam pressing the entire panel.
4. Repeat steps 1–3 to construct the remaining 6 panels.

Assembling the Quilt Top

1. Sew the sixteen 3" x 42" cream solid sashing strips end to end to create a single 3"-wide strip. Crosscut this strip into eight 3" x 60½" strips for horizontal sashing, and two 3" x 79½" strips for vertical sashing.
2. Refer to the assembly diagram on page 27 and the quilt photo on page 22. Lay out the pieced panels and sashing strips as shown, including the 3" x 79½" vertical sashing strips. With right sides together, and matching ends and midpoints, sew the panels and sashing strips together, finishing with the side or vertical sashing strips. Press all seams toward the sashing strips.
3. Sew the nine 12½" x 42" dark teal border strips end to end to create a single 12½"-wide strip. Refer to "Adding Borders" on page 40 for guidance as needed with measuring the quilt top, and cut border strips of the appropriate lengths from the long 12½"-wide strip. Sew the strips to your quilt, sewing the top and bottom border strips first, and then the side strips. Press the seams toward the borders.

Finishing

Refer to "Finishing Techniques" on pages 40–44 for guidance as needed with marking, basting, quilting, and finishing your quilt.

1. Divide the backing fabric crosswise into 3 equal panels of approximately 93" each. Remove the selvages and join the pieces to make a single, large backing panel.
2. Position the backing fabric so the seams run horizontally. Center and layer the quilt top and the batting over the backing; baste.
3. Quilt as desired. Depending on the fabric you choose, the borders can present a wonderful opportunity to be creative with your quilting.
4. Trim the batting and backing even with the edges of the quilt top.
5. Use the 2½" x 42" strips to make the binding. Sew the binding to the quilt, adding a hanging sleeve if desired.
6. Make a label and attach it to your quilt.

THE MONOGRAM QUILT

The Monogram Quilt by Terry Martin, 2000, Snohomish, Washington, 95" x 104". Quilted by Barbara Dau.

A beautiful alphabet by Anne Orr was the inspiration for this quilt. Use neutral colors for a more masculine look.

I really enjoyed designing this quilt; it was one of those projects that kept me lying awake at night. I think you'll agree that a monogram is a great way to personalize a quilt.

I modified a charted alphabet designed by Anne Orr in the Dover book *Anne Orr's Charted Designs* and designed the quilt around my last-name initial—*M*. I introduced the oval frame but realized quickly that there would still be a tremendous amount of background area. If I used solid-colored fabric both inside and outside the oval and added a wide border, there would be too much "blank" space for my taste (although it would be a great opportunity for quilting). I also wanted the quilt to have a masculine flavor so that it would be pleasing to my husband. With a little additional research, I discovered the traditional Plaid block and felt it was a good choice for the background inside the oval frame. (If you prefer to use just one fabric, substitute a total of 3¼ yards for the 7 different fabrics that I suggest.) I think the blue printed fabric outside the oval adds depth and texture. Once I found the solid-colored fabrics for the flowers outside the monogram that perfectly matched the outside border, I was set to go.

Quilt Size: 95" x 104"

Materials

42" wide fabrics; 44"-wide (minimum) gridded, fusible interfacing

Note: Yardages for both the Plaid block background (inside the oval, fabrics #1–#7) and the monogram (dark blue solid) will depend upon the letter you select from the alphabet chart provided on pages 36–39. Yardage and cutting information for each letter is provided in the chart. Yardage and cutting information for the corresponding Plaid block background is referenced in the project instructions under "Cutting for the Pieced Panels" on pages 29–30.

6 yds. lightweight, gridded, fusible interfacing

¾ yds. dark green solid for oval frame and rosebud greenery in background (outside the oval)

3 yds. subtle blue print for background (outside the oval) and inner border

Scraps of light pink and dark pink solids for rosebuds in background (outside the oval)

⅛ yd. medium pink solid for rosebuds in background (outside the oval)

¾ yd. red solid for middle border and corner blocks

3½ yds. floral plaid for outer border and corner blocks

8¼ yds. fabric for backing

¾ yd. fabric for binding*

**I used the same floral plaid as I used for the outer border.*

Cutting for the Pieced Panels

This quilt is based on 1" finished squares. Cut all strips 1½" x 42", which includes ¼"-wide seam allowance.

Monogram

See "Alphabet Chart" (pages 36–39) for yardages and cutting instructions for your choice of letter. Cut the appropriate number of 1½" squares from a dark blue solid fabric.

Plaid Block Background (Inside the Oval)

See the note on page 29. A diagram of a single Plaid block, with fabric key, is provided below for reference.

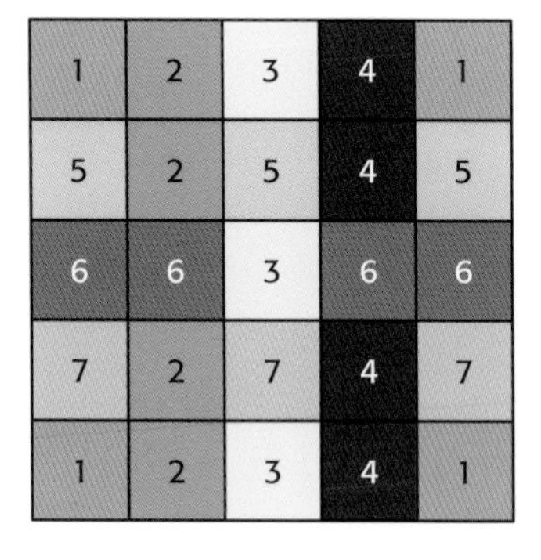

There are approximately 72 Plaid blocks surrounding the monogram and contained within the dark green oval. (This number takes into account both the complete blocks and the partial blocks along the oval's edges.) The exact number of Plaid blocks and the exact yardage required for the 7 different Plaid block fabrics will depend upon the monogram you choose. The fabric quantities listed here are for all 72 Plaid blocks, with no subtraction made for the monogram letter. Obviously this will be more fabric than you need, though not by much. I feel it is important to give you a reasonable estimate for each of the fabrics; it is always better to have a little extra than not enough!

If you don't want too many leftover squares, simply cut about three-quarters of the number of strips required for each color. You can always cut more strips and squares if you need them. If you'd rather know the exact number of strips and squares that you will need for the Plaid blocks around your monogram, skip the following cutting instructions and cut strips and squares after you read "Designing Your Monogram" on page 31.

FABRIC	YARDAGE	TOTAL NUMBER OF STRIPS	TOTAL NUMBER OF SQUARES
#1 Blue	⅝ yd.	11	288
#2 Pink	⅝ yd.	11	288
#3 Cream	½ yd.	8	216
#4 Red	⅝ yd.	11	288
#5 Yellow	½ yd.	8	216
#6 Dark gold	⅝ yd.	11	288
#7 Green	½ yd.	8	216

Oval Frame

FABRIC	TOTAL NUMBER OF STRIPS	TOTAL NUMBER OF SQUARES
Dark green	11	282

Background (Outside the Oval)

FABRIC	TOTAL NUMBER OF STRIPS	TOTAL NUMBER OF SQUARES
Dark green	3	84
Subtle blue print	49	1349
Light pink	n/a	12
Medium pink	1	24
Dark pink	n/a	12

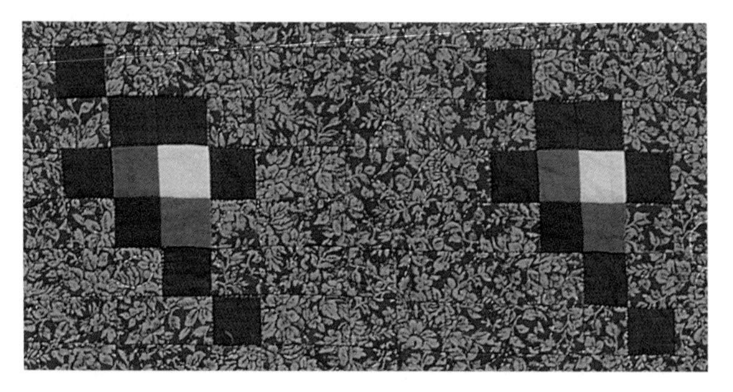

Colorful rosebuds add visual interest in the subtle blue background.

Cutting Interfacing, Borders, and Binding

From the gridded, fusible interfacing, cut:
Four pieces, each 43½" x 51", for the pieced panels

From the remaining subtle blue print, cut:
7 strips, each 3½" x 42", for inner border

From the red solid, cut:
10 strips, each 2½" x 42", for middle border and corner blocks

From the floral plaid, cut:
8 strips, each 14½" x 42", for outer border and corner blocks

From the binding fabric, cut:
10 strips, each 2½" x 42"

Designing Your Monogram

My quilt features my monogram—the letter *M*—as its centerpiece. Of course, you'll want to replace my monogram with your own in the center of your quilt. It's easy!

1. Make an enlarged black-and-white photocopy of the illustration on page 32, which indicates the placement of the Plaid blocks within the dark green oval frame. (Enlarge to any size that is easy for you to work with.) The black **X** marks the center of the charted design. You'll also notice that the charted design is divided vertically and horizontally, into 4 sections or quadrants. I'll explain more about these divisions later on in the project.
2. Refer to the alphabet chart on pages 36–39 and find the letter you wish to use. You'll notice that each letter is marked with a black **X** in the center square. This marked square corresponds to the center square on the charted design you photocopied in step 1.
3. Beginning with the marked center square, use a pencil to transfer your letter design to the photocopied design from step 1. Work square by square, filling in each square necessary to complete your monogram. You'll use this complete chart as your personal guide for laying out and constructing the pieced panels (see "Layout and Construction of the Pieced Panels" on page 33).
4. Remember those vertical and horizontal lines we mentioned back in step 1? These indicate the 4 separate panels you'll be constructing to complete the charted portion of the quilt top. You may find it helpful to actually cut your complete chart from step 3 into 4 sections, which will keep you focused on the panel you are working on without the distraction of the entire design. If you'd rather not cut the chart, mark over the dividing lines with a colored pencil or marker.
5. Based on your complete chart, determine the number of squares you'll need from fabrics #1–#7 for the Plaid background. Refer to "Figuring Yardage" on page 17 to calculate the necessary yardages, and cut the appropriate number of strips and squares from each fabric.

Substitute your monogram for the M *in the center of my quilt. See the alphabet chart on pages 36–39.*

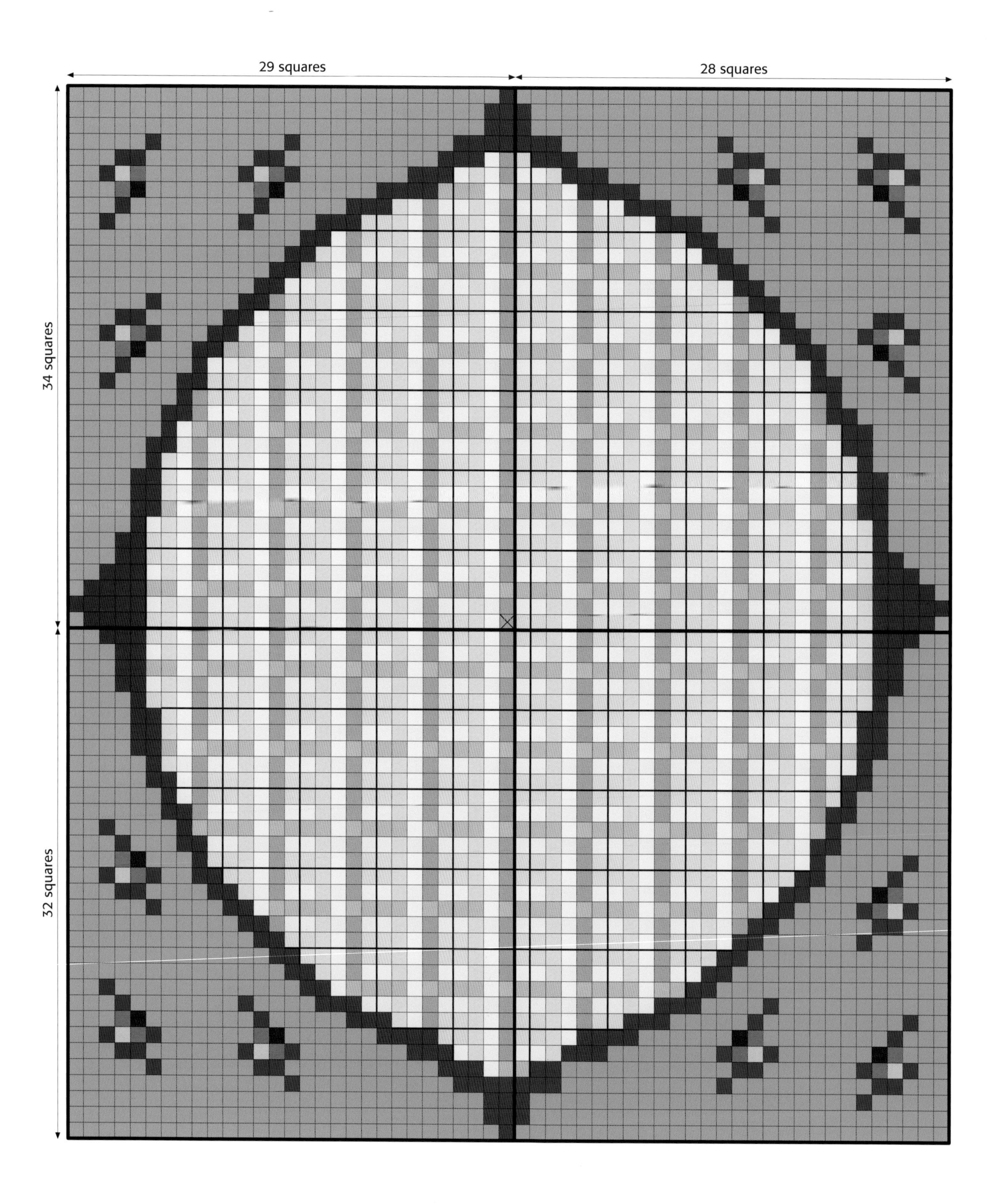
29 squares
28 squares
34 squares
32 squares

Layout and Construction of the Pieced Panels

Note: Refer to "Basic Techniques for Cross-Stitch Quilts" on pages 7–16 for guidance as needed. The center portion of the quilt (charted monogram and background) is composed of 4 separately constructed panels. Follow the instructions below to construct each panel. Begin with the lower right-hand panel.

1. Spread a 43½" x 51" piece of gridded interfacing, fusible side up, on your ironing surface. To make the most efficient use of the fusible interfacing, run the lengthwise edges *vertically* for this project.
2. Begin in the lower right-hand corner of the fusible interfacing. Position the squares (and strips if you are using them) as shown on your personal monogram chart, carefully aligning the pieces with the vertical and horizontal lines on the grid. Stop periodically to press the pieces to the fusible interfacing as you go, following the manufacturer's instructions regarding iron temperature, use of steam, and so on.
3. When the entire panel has been laid out and fused, stitch the vertical and horizontal seams as described in "Sewing the Seams" on pages 13–14. Finish by steam pressing the entire panel.
4. Repeat steps 1–3 to complete each of the remaining 3 panels.
5. Arrange the 4 panels as indicated in your complete monogram chart. Since sizes of the pieced panels vary slightly, you'll have excess interfacing around some of the panel edges. Trim the excess interfacing even with the panel edges. With right sides together and pinning carefully to match the seams, sew the panels together in pairs. Press the seams as desired.
6. Sew the 2 panels from step 5 together to complete the design; press.

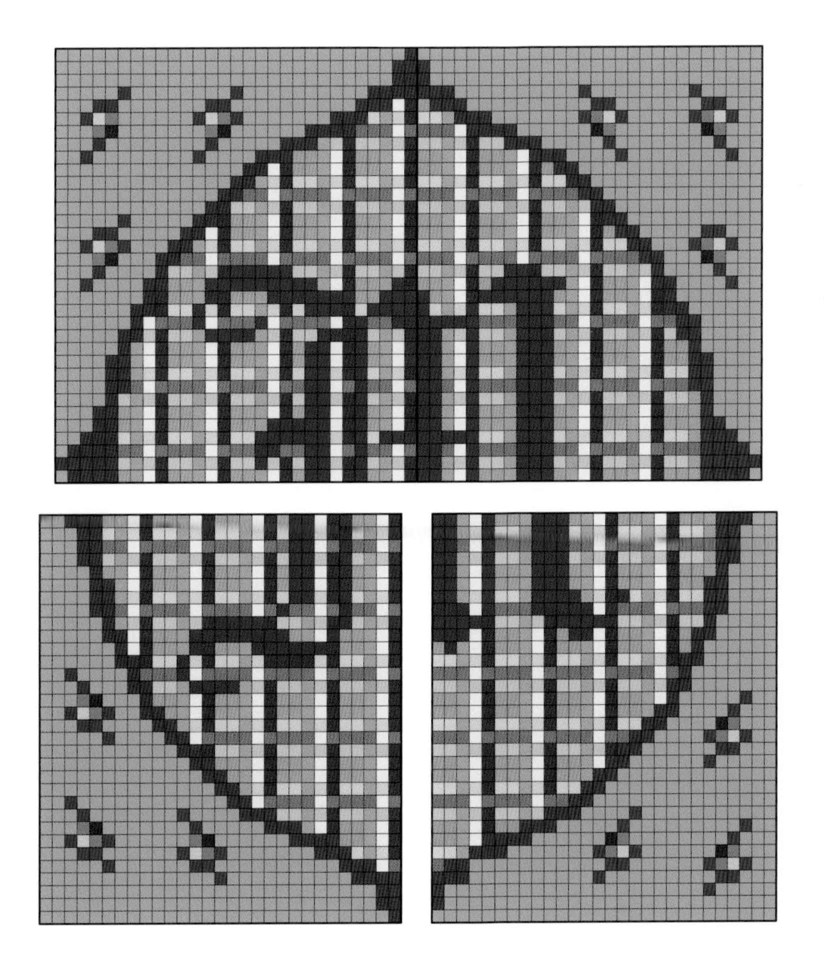

Adding Borders

1. Sew the seven 3½" x 42" blue-print inner border strips end to end to create a single 3½"-wide strip. Refer to "Adding Borders" on page 40 for guidance as needed with measuring the quilt top, cutting borders of the appropriate lengths from the long 3½"-wide strip, and sewing these strips to your quilt. Add borders to the sides first; then add the top and bottom borders to the quilt. Press the seams toward the borders.
2. Sew 5 of the 2½" x 42" red solid middle-border strips end to end to create a single 2½"-wide strip. Repeat with 5 of the 14½" x 42" floral plaid outer border strips to create a single 14½"-wide strip.
3. With right sides together and long raw edges aligned, sew the 2½"-wide red solid strip and the 14½"-wide floral plaid strip from step 2 together to make a single border unit. Press the seam toward the red solid strip.

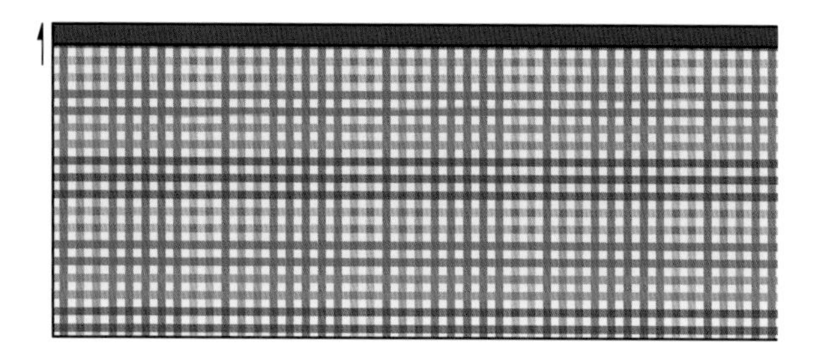

4. Refer to "Adding Borders" on page 40. Measure the quilt through its vertical center. Cut 2 border strips to this measurement from the border unit you created in step 3; sew these strips to the sides of the quilt. Be sure to position the red solid strips closest to the quilt center.
5. Cut four 14½" segments from the remaining border unit from step 3. Set these segments aside for the corner blocks.

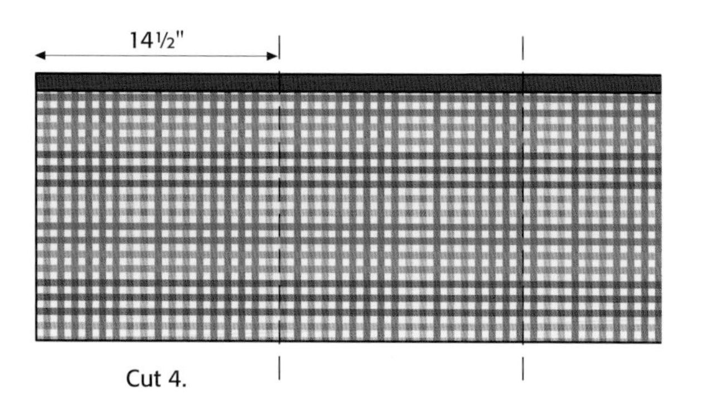

Cut 4.

6. Sew the remaining five 2½" x 42" red solid strips end to end as in step 2 to create another single 2½"-wide strip. Repeat with the remaining three 14½" x 42" floral plaid strips.
7. Measure the quilt through its horizontal center to the outer edges of the blue inner border and add ½" for seam allowances. Cut 2 outer border strips to this measurement from the 14½"-wide floral plaid strip sewn in step 6.
8. Sew a corner block from step 5 to the short end of each 14½"-wide floral outer border strip cut in step 7 as shown. Press the seams toward the corner blocks.

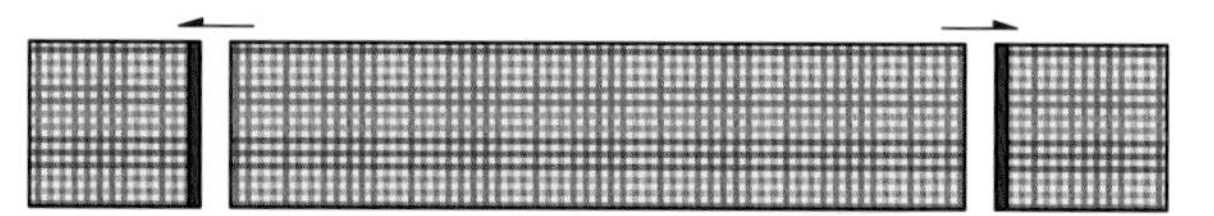

Make 2.

9. Measure the quilt through its horizontal center, including all borders. Cut 2 strips to this measurement from the 2½"-wide red solid strip sewn in step 6. Sew one of these red solid strips to each of the floral outer border units sewn in step 8, creating a top and bottom border unit as shown. Press the seams toward the red solid strips.

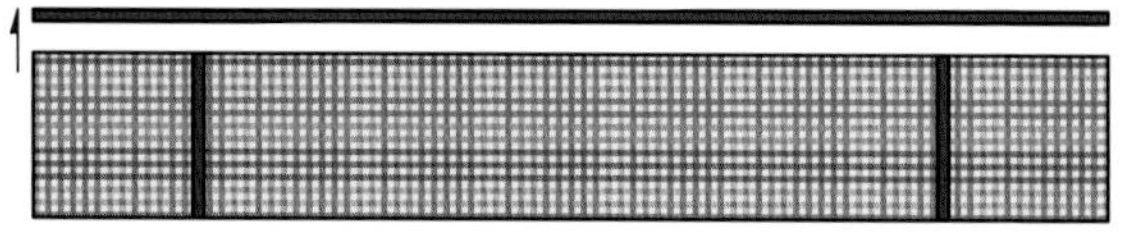

Make 2.

10. With right sides together and pinning carefully to match ends, centers, and seams, sew the top and bottom borders to the quilt. Be sure to position the red solid strips closest to the quilt center. Press the seams toward the borders.

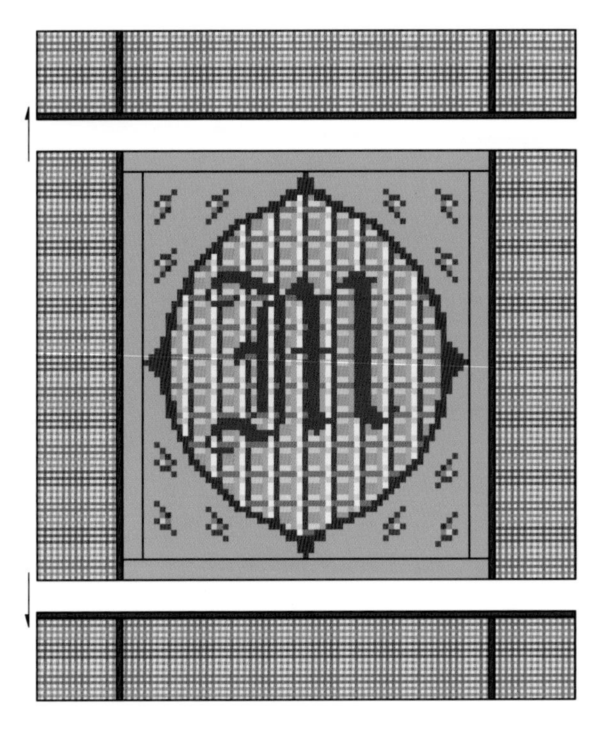

Finishing

Refer to "Finishing Techniques" on pages 40–44 for guidance as needed with marking, basting, quilting, and finishing your quilt.

1. Divide the backing fabric crosswise into 3 equal panels of approximately 100" each. Remove the selvages and join the pieces to make a single, large backing panel.
2. Position the backing fabric so the seams run horizontally. Center and layer the quilt top and the batting over the backing; baste.
3. Quilt as desired. Depending on the fabric you choose, the borders can present a wonderful opportunity to be creative with your quilting.
4. Trim the batting and backing even with the edges of the quilt top.
5. Use the 2½" x 42" strips to make the binding. Sew the binding to the quilt, adding a hanging sleeve if desired.
6. Make a label and attach it to your quilt.

Alphabet Chart

Note: Cut all strips 1½" wide.

Monogram Initial	Yardage	Total Number of Strips	Total Number of Squares
A	⅜ yd.	7	194
B	½ yd.	9	226
C	⅜ yd.	7	191
D	½ yd.	9	224
E	⅜ yd.	8	209
F	½ yd.	9	226
G	½ yd.	9	239
H	½ yd.	10	262
I	⅜ yd.	7	179
J	⅜ yd.	7	180
K	½ yd.	9	228
L	⅜ yd.	8	208
M	⅝ yd.	12	321
N	⅜ yd.	8	216
O	½ yd.	9	236
P	½ yd.	10	278
Q	½ yd.	10	265
R	⅜ yd.	8	205
S	½ yd.	9	249
T	½ yd.	9	224
U	⅜ yd.	8	204
V	⅜ yd.	7	179
W	⅝ yd.	13	360
X	⅜ yd.	6	153
Y	⅜ yd.	8	202
Z	⅜ yd.	7	188

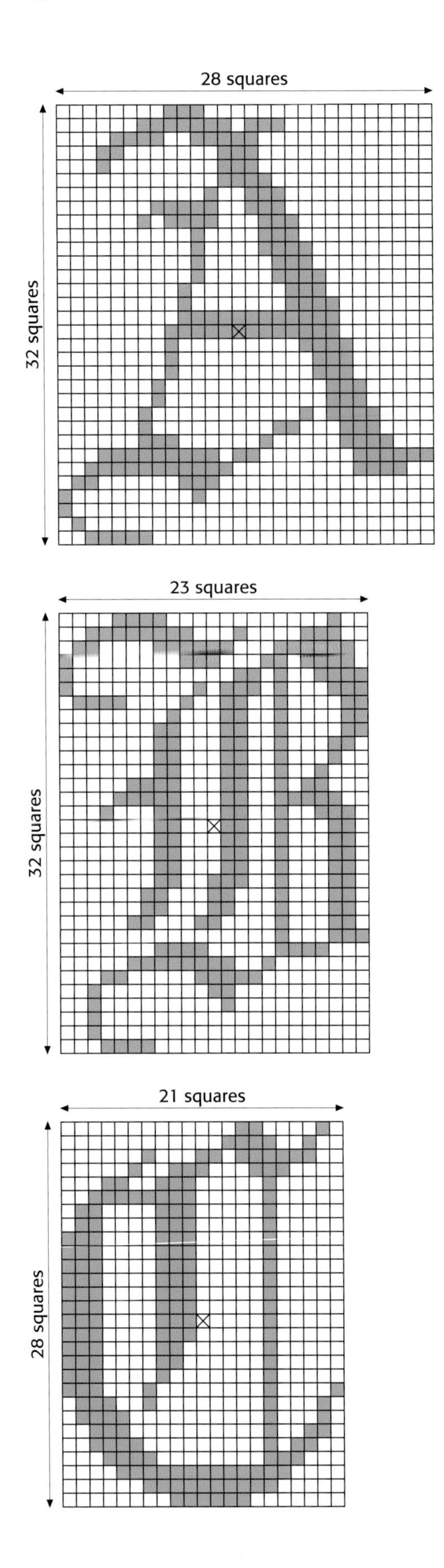

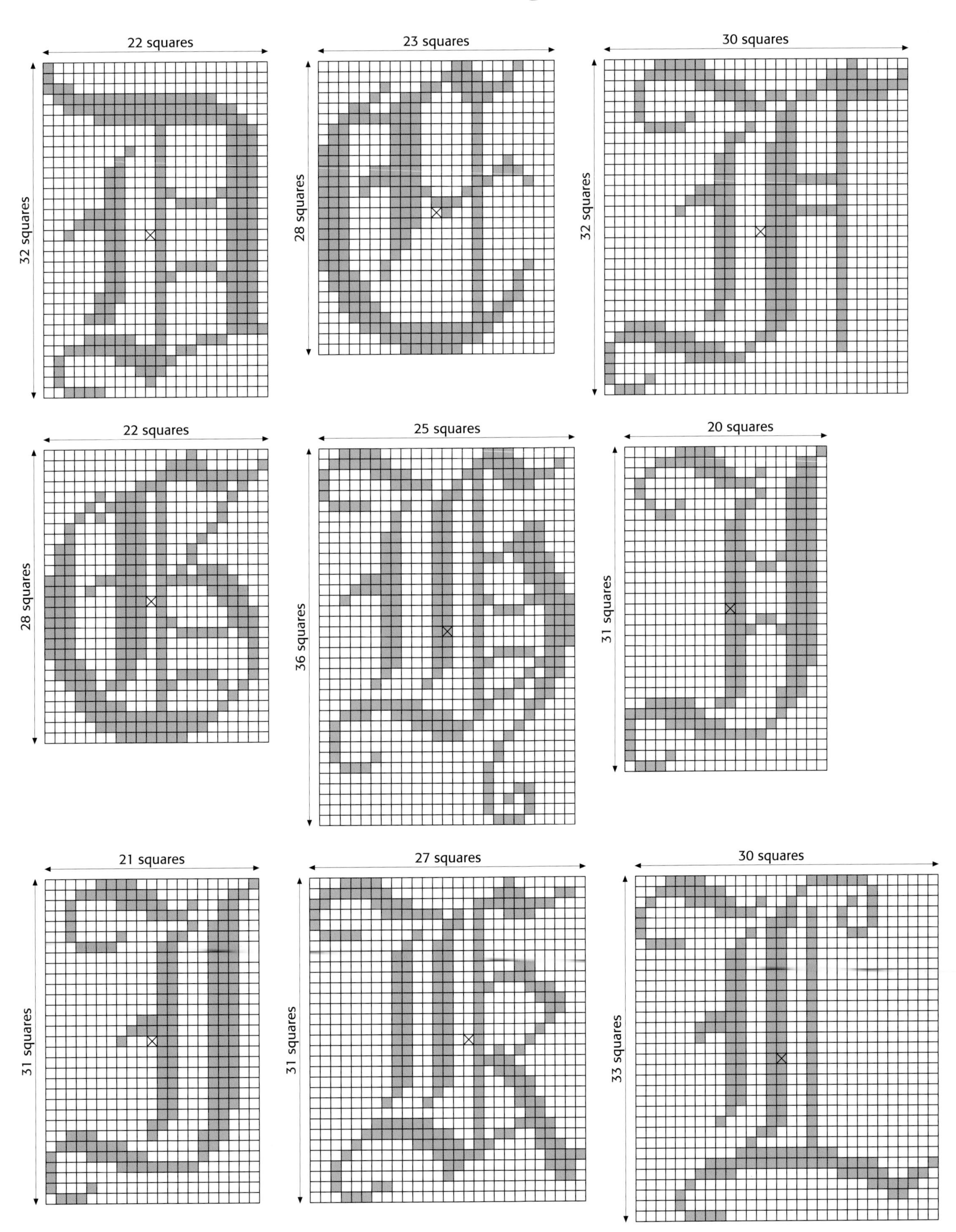
22 squares
32 squares
23 squares
28 squares
30 squares
32 squares
22 squares
28 squares
25 squares
36 squares
20 squares
31 squares
21 squares
31 squares
27 squares
31 squares
30 squares
33 squares

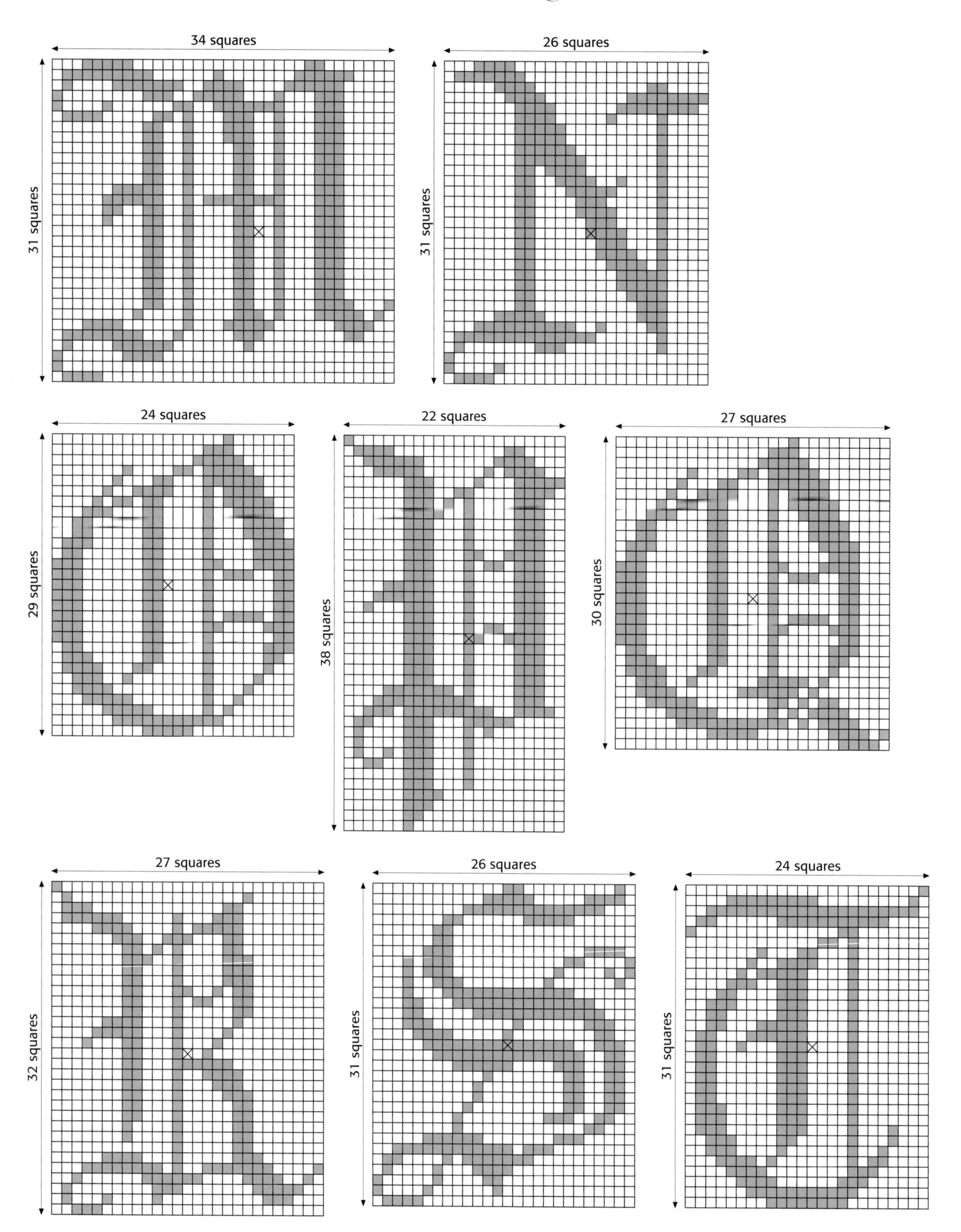
34 squares
31 squares
26 squares
31 squares
24 squares
29 squares
22 squares
38 squares
27 squares
30 squares
27 squares
32 squares
26 squares
31 squares
24 squares
31 squares

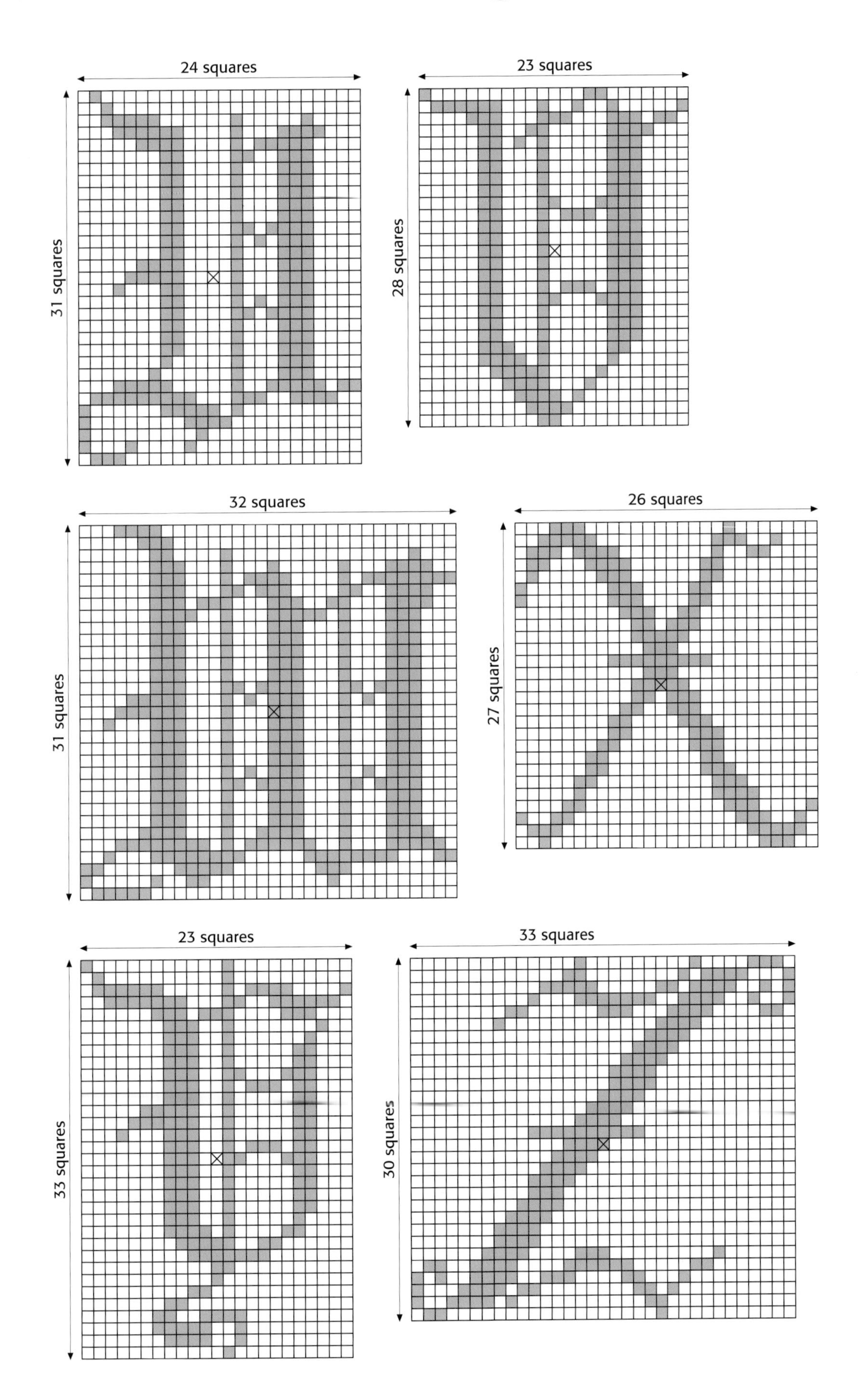
24 squares
31 squares
23 squares
28 squares
32 squares
31 squares
26 squares
27 squares
23 squares
33 squares
33 squares
30 squares

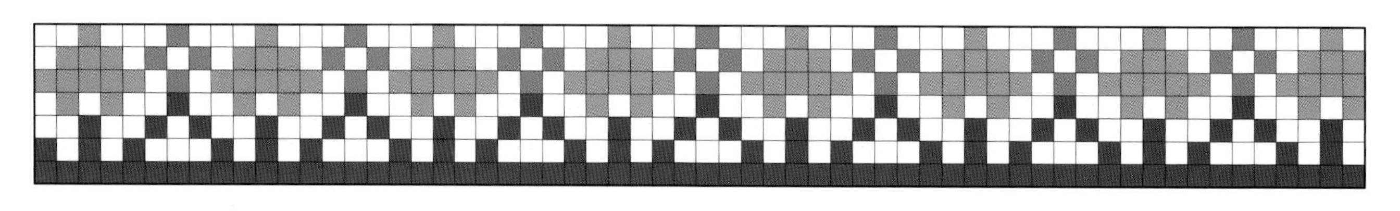

Finishing Techniques

Adding Borders

All of the quilts in this book are made with straight-cut (rather than mitered) borders. For best results, do not cut border strips and sew them directly to the quilt sides without measuring first. The edges of a quilt often measure slightly longer than the distance through the quilt center, due to stretching during construction. Therefore, measure the quilt top through the center in both directions, as explained in the steps below, to determine how long to cut the border strips. Measuring this way ensures that the finished quilt will be as straight and as "square" as possible, without wavy edges. Also, sew a standard ¼"-wide seam allowance when adding borders.

Plain border strips are commonly cut along the crosswise grain and seamed where extra length is needed. Borders cut from the lengthwise grain of fabric require extra yardage, but seaming the required length is then unnecessary.

1. Measure the width of the quilt top through the center. Cut border strips to that measurement, piecing as necessary. Mark the center of the top and bottom quilt edges and the border strips. Pin the borders to the top and bottom edges of the quilt top, matching the center marks and ends and easing as necessary. Sew the border strips in place. Press seams toward the border.

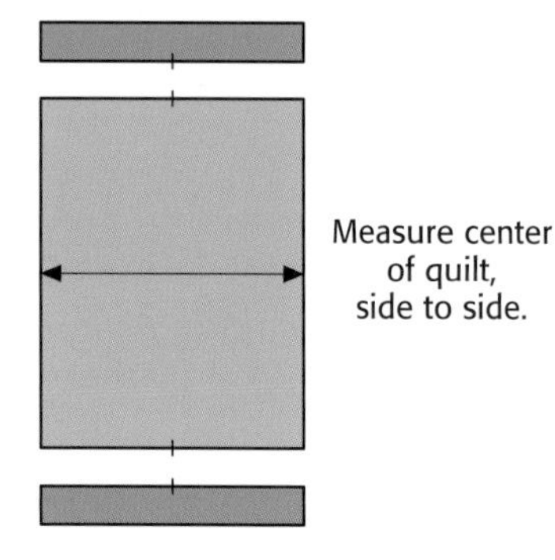

Mark centers.

2. Measure the length of the quilt top through the center, including the top and bottom border strips just added. Cut border strips to that measurement, piecing as necessary; mark the center of the quilt edges and the border strips. Pin the border strips to the sides of the quilt top, matching the center marks and ends and easing as necessary; stitch. Press seams toward the border.

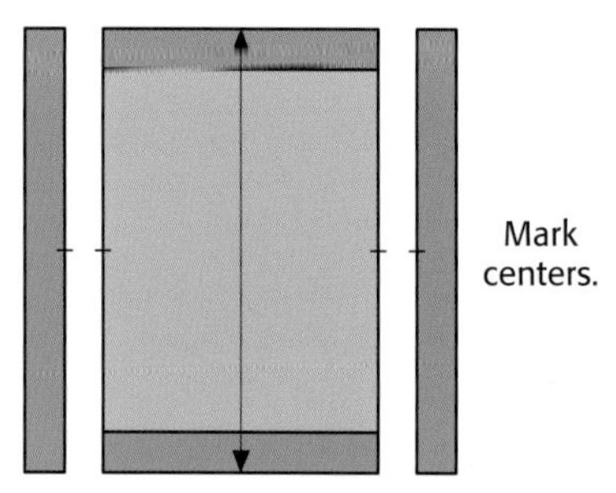

Measure center of quilt, top to bottom, including borders.

Preparing to Quilt

Marking the Quilting Lines

Whether or not to mark the quilting designs depends upon the type of quilting you will be doing. Marking is not necessary if you plan to quilt in the ditch, outline quilt a uniform distance from seam lines, or free-motion quilt by machine in a random pattern. For more complex quilting designs, or for straight lines and grids, mark the quilt top before the quilt is layered with batting and backing.

Choose a marking tool that will be visible on your fabric and test it on fabric scraps to be sure the marks can be removed easily. Masking tape can be used to mark straight quilting lines. Tape only small sections at a time and remove the tape when you stop at the end of the day; otherwise, the sticky residue may be difficult to remove from the fabric.

Layering the Quilt

The quilt "sandwich" consists of backing, batting, and the quilt top. Cut the quilt backing at least 4" larger than the quilt top all the way around. For large quilts, it is usually necessary to sew two or three lengths of fabric together to make a backing of the required size. (You'll find this information in the individual project instructions when applicable.) Trim away the selvages before piecing the lengths together, and press seams open to make quilting easier.

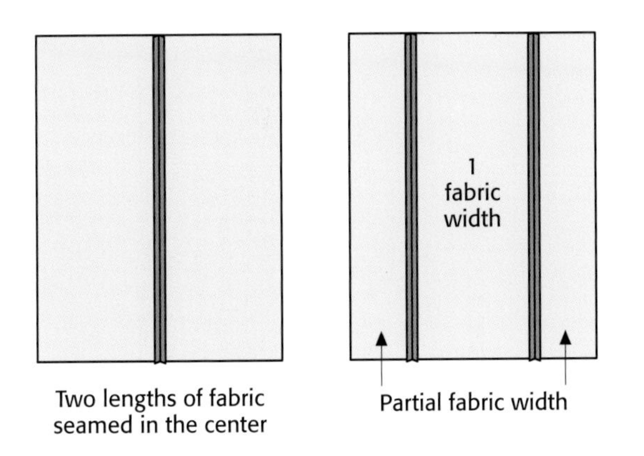

Two lengths of fabric seamed in the center

Partial fabric width

Batting comes packaged in standard bed sizes, or it can be purchased by the yard. Several weights or thicknesses are available. Thick battings are fine for tied quilts and comforters; a thinner batting is better, however, if you intend to quilt rather than tie the finished quilt top.

To put all the layers together, follow these steps:

1. Spread the backing, wrong side up, on a flat, clean surface. Anchor it with pins or masking tape. Be careful not to stretch the backing out of shape.
2. Spread the batting over the backing, smoothing out any wrinkles.
3. Place the pressed quilt top on top of the batting. Smooth out any wrinkles and make sure the quilt-top edges are parallel to the edges of the backing.
4. Starting in the center, baste with needle and thread; work diagonally to each corner. Continue basting in a grid of horizontal and vertical lines 6" to 8" apart. Finish by basting around the edges.

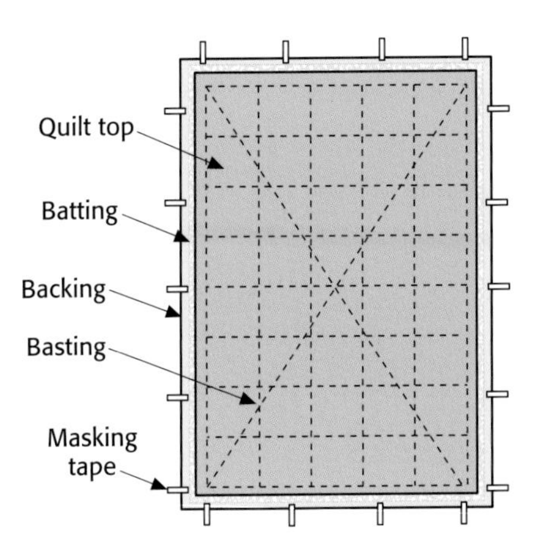

Note: For machine quilting, you may baste the layers with #2 rustproof safety pins. Place pins about 6" to 8" apart, away from the areas you intend to quilt.

Hand Quilting

Given the added layer of interfacing and the many seams involved, the pieced panel areas of these quilts do not lend themselves to hand quilting. (See "A Word about Quilting" on page 16.) However, each quilt also includes large borders that are not pieced and provide an excellent "canvas" for the hand quilter.

To quilt by hand, you will need short, sturdy needles called "Betweens," quilting thread, and a thimble to fit the middle finger of your sewing hand. Most quilters also use a frame or hoop to support their work. Use the smallest needle you can comfortably handle; the finer the needle, the smaller your stitches will be.

1. Thread your needle with a single strand of quilting thread about 18" long. Make a small knot and insert the needle in the top layer about 1" from the place where you want to start stitching. Pull the needle out at the point where quilting will begin, and gently pull the thread until the knot pops through the fabric and into the batting.
2. Take small, evenly spaced stitches through all 3 quilt layers. Rock the needle up and down through all layers, until you have 3 or 4 stitches on the needle. Place your other hand underneath the quilt so you can feel the needle point with the tip of your finger when a stitch is taken.
3. To end a line of quilting, make a small knot close to the last stitch. Backstitch, running the thread a needle's length through the batting. Gently pull the thread until the knot pops into the batting; clip the thread at the quilt's surface.

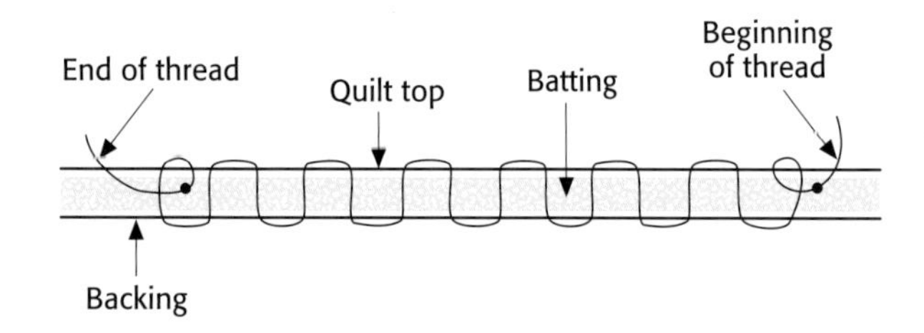

Machine Quilting

Machine quilting is suitable for all types of quilts, from crib to full-size bed quilts. With machine quilting, you can quickly complete quilts that might otherwise languish on the shelves.

For straight-line quilting, it is extremely helpful to have a walking foot to help feed the quilt layers through the machine without shifting or puckering. Some machines have a built-in walking foot; other machines require a separate attachment.

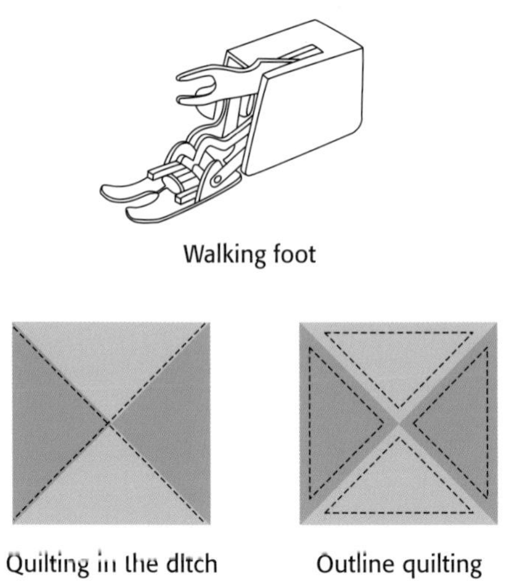

Walking foot

Quilting in the ditch

Outline quilting

For free-motion quilting, you'll need a darning foot and the ability to drop the feed dogs on your machine. With free-motion quilting, you do not turn the fabric under the needle but instead guide the fabric in the direction of the design. Use free-motion quilting to outline-quilt a fabric motif or to create stippling or other curved designs.

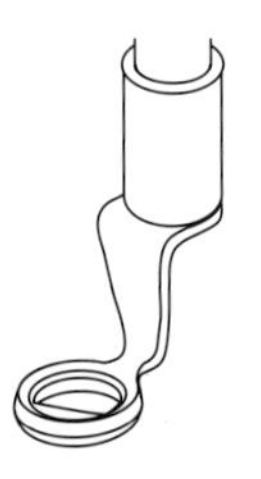

Darning foot

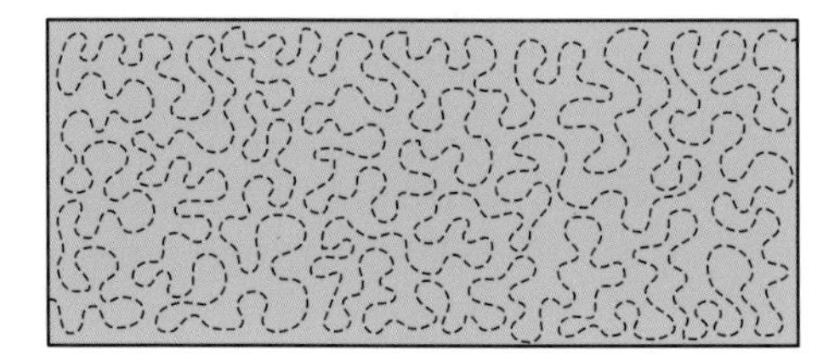

Free-motion quilting

Binding

Bindings can be made from straight-grain or bias-grain strips of fabric. For a French double-fold binding, cut strips 2½" wide across the width of the fabric. You will need enough strips to go around the perimeter of the quilt plus 10" for seams and the corners in a mitered fold.

1. Join strips at right angles, right sides together, and stitch across the corner as shown to make a single, long length of binding. Trim excess fabric and press the seams open.

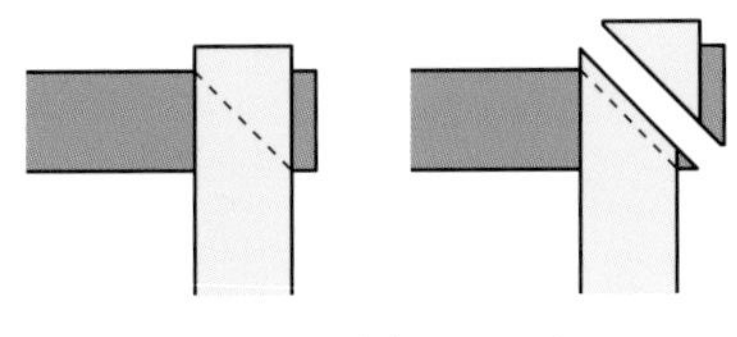

Joining straight-cut strips

2. Fold the strip in half lengthwise, wrong sides together, and press. Trim one end of the strip at a 45° angle and turn under ¼"; press. Trimming and turning the end under at an angle distributes the bulk so you won't have a lump where the two ends of the binding meet.

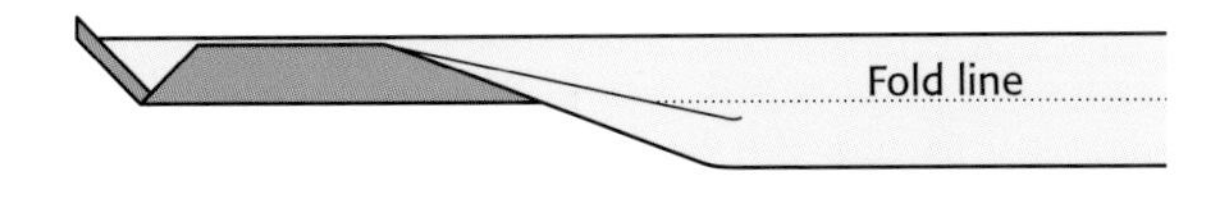

3. Trim the batting and backing even with the quilt top. If you plan to add a sleeve, do so now before attaching the binding (see "Adding a Sleeve" on page 44).
4. Starting on one side of the quilt and using a ⅜"-wide seam allowance, stitch the binding to the quilt. Keep the raw edges even with the quilt-top edge. End the stitching ⅜" from the first corner of the quilt; backstitch. Clip the thread.

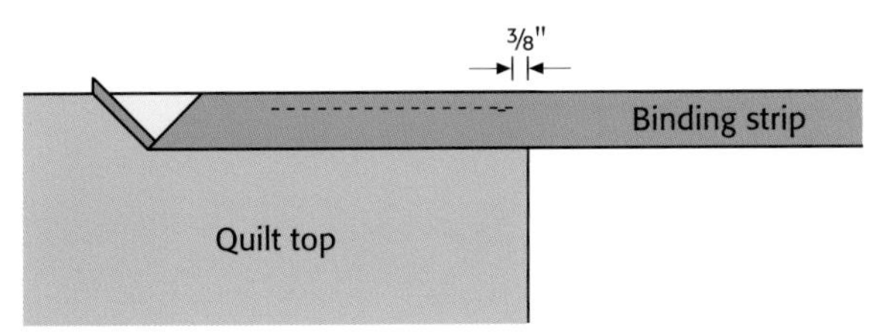

5. Turn the quilt so that you'll be stitching down the next side. Fold the binding up, away from the quilt, then back down onto itself, parallel with the edge of the quilt top. Begin stitching at the edge, backstitching to secure. Repeat on the remaining edges and corners of the quilt.

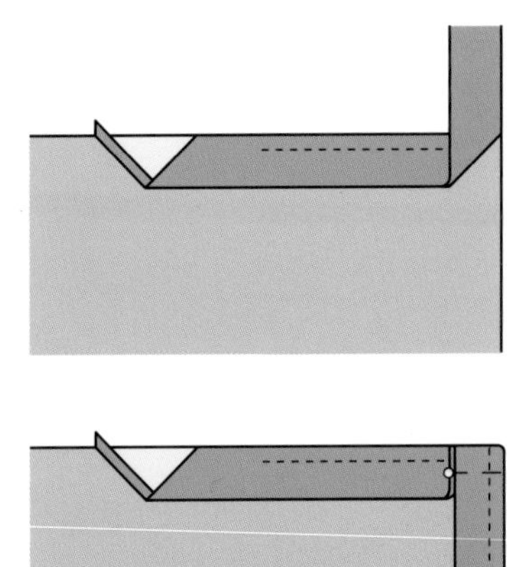

6. When you are several inches from the beginning of the binding, stop stitching. Overlap the beginning of the binding 1" with the loose end of the binding; cut away any excess and trim the end at a 45° angle. Tuck the end of the binding into the fold at the beginning of the binding and finish the seam.

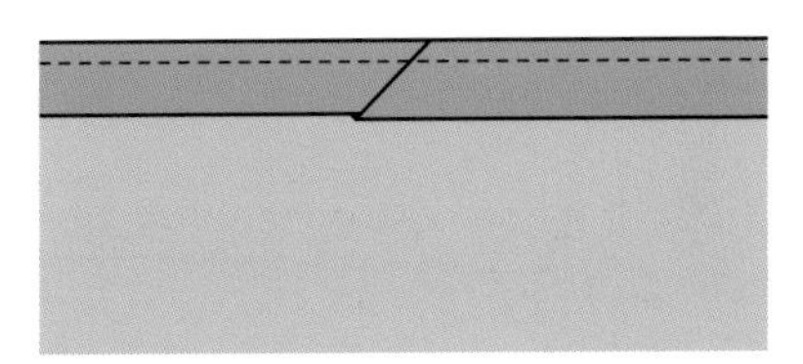

7. Fold the binding over the raw edges of the quilt to the back, with the folded edge covering the row of machine stitching, and blindstitch in place. A miter will form at each corner. Blindstitch the mitered corners.

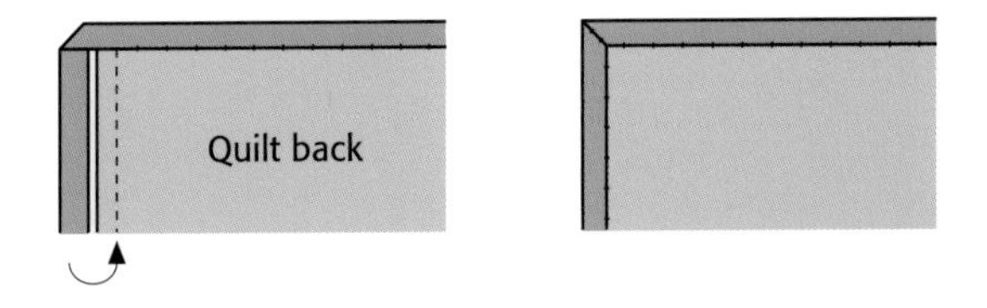

Adding a Sleeve

If you plan to display your finished quilt on the wall, be sure to add a hanging sleeve to hold the rod.

1. Using leftover fabric from the front (or a piece of muslin), cut a strip 6" to 8" wide and 1" shorter than the width of the quilt's top edge. Fold the short ends under ½", and then ½" again; stitch.

2. Fold the fabric strip in half lengthwise, wrong sides together, and baste the raw edges to the top edge of the quilt back. The top edge of the sleeve will be secured when the binding is sewn on the quilt.

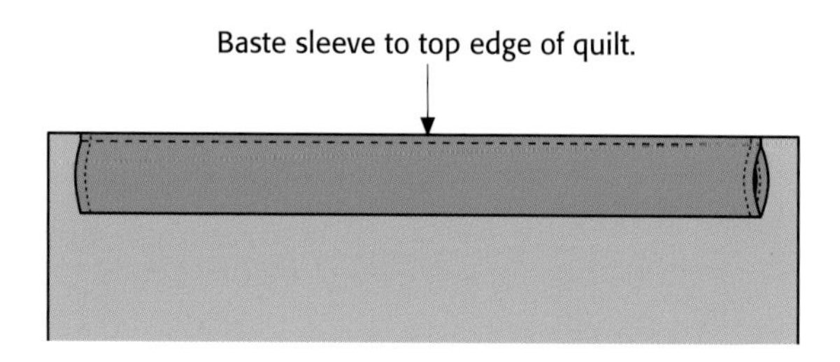

3. Finish the sleeve after the binding has been attached by blindstitching the bottom of the sleeve in place. Push the bottom edge of the sleeve up just a bit to provide a little give so the hanging rod does not put strain on the quilt itself.

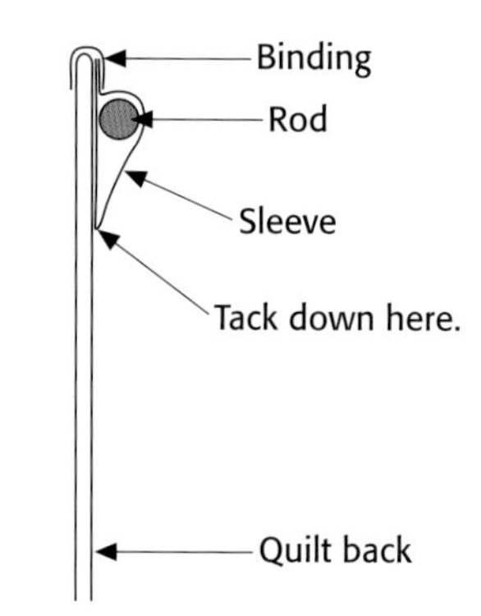

Signing Your Quilt

Be sure to sign and date your quilt. Future generations will be interested to know more than just who made it and when. Labels can be as elaborate or as simple as you desire. The information can be handwritten, typed, or embroidered. Be sure to include the name of the quilt, your name, your city and state, the date, the name of the recipient if the quilt is a gift, and any other interesting or important information about the quilt.

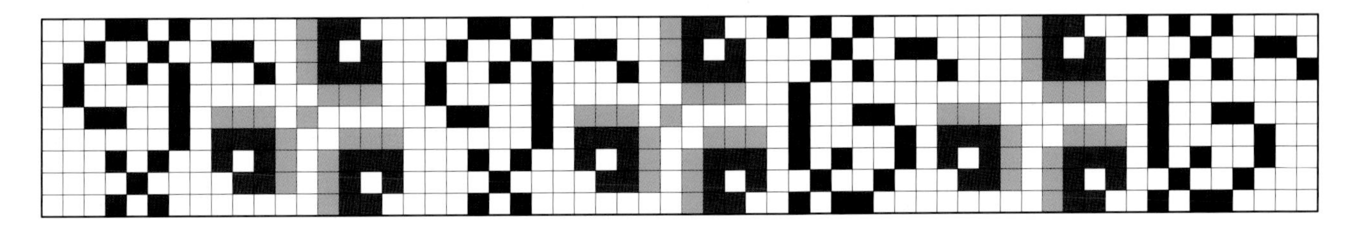

Resources

Dover Publications
21 East 2nd Street
Mineola, NY 11501
www.DoverPublications.com
Great copyright-free materials

Freudenberg Pellon Nonwovens
3440 Industrial Drive
Eno Industrial Park
Durham, NC 27704
919-620-3942
800-223-5275
Lightweight, gridded, fusible interfacing

HTC, Inc.
103 Eisenhower Parkway
Roseland, NJ 07068
973-618-9380
888-618-2555
www.htc-inc.net
Lightweight, gridded, fusible interfacing

Quiltsmart Printed Interfacing
PO Box 1008
Chanhassen, MN 55317
952-445-5737
888-446-5750
info@quiltsmart.com
Lightweight, gridded, fusible interfacing

RJR Fashion Fabrics
800-422-5426
www.rjrfabrics.com
Fabulous, 100 percent–cotton sateen fabric

Bibliography

Anne Orr's Charted Designs. New York: Dover Publications, Inc., 1978.

Favorite Charted Designs by Anne Orr. New York: Dover Publications, Inc., 1983.

Houck, Carter, ed. *101 Folk Art Designs for Counted Cross-Stitch and Other Needlecrafts.* New York: Dover Publications, Inc., 1982.

Pappas, Dina. *Quick Watercolor Quilts.* Bothell, Wash.: That Patchwork Place, 1999.

Waldvogel, Merikay. *Soft Covers for Hard Times.* Nashville, Tenn.: Rutledge Hill Press, 1990.

Woodard, Thomas K., and Blanche Greenstein. *Twentieth Century Quilts 1900–1950.* New York: E. P. Dutton, 1988.

Practice Motifs and Graph Paper

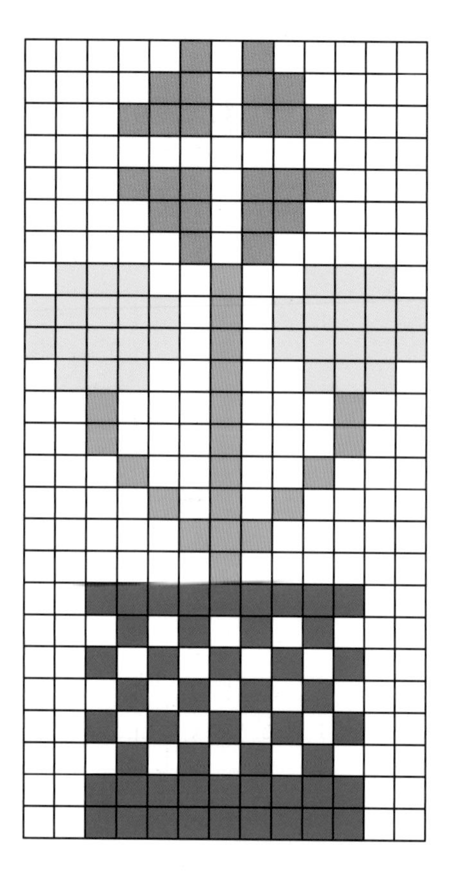

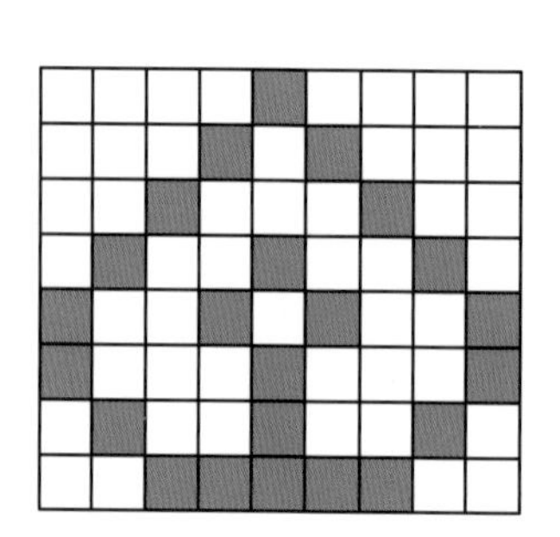

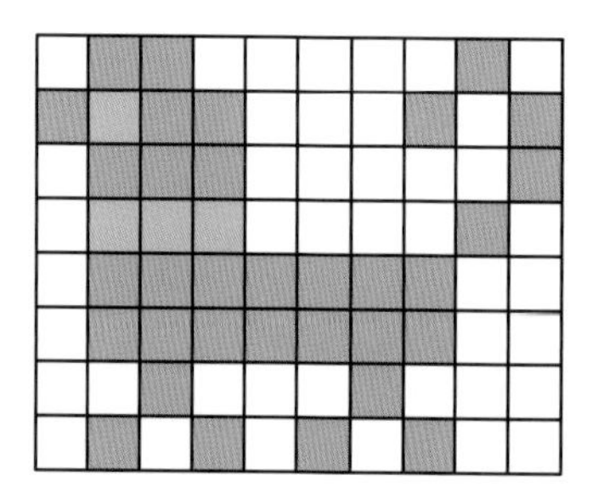

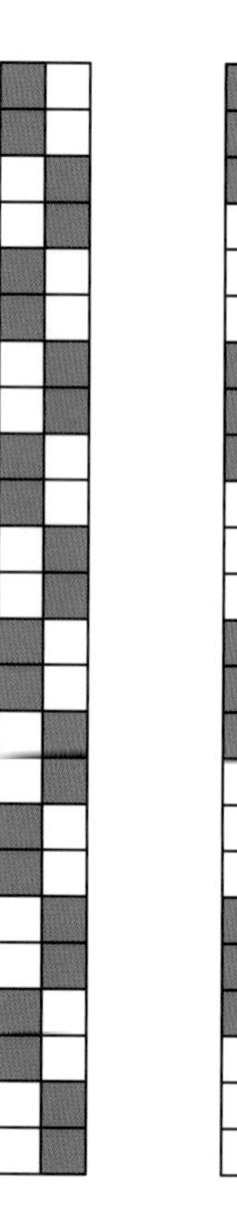

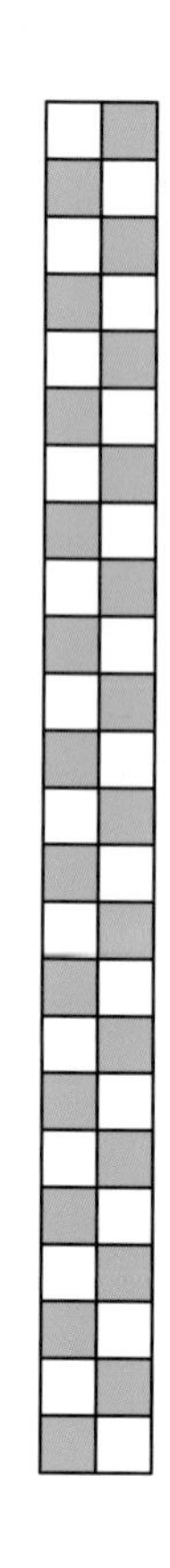

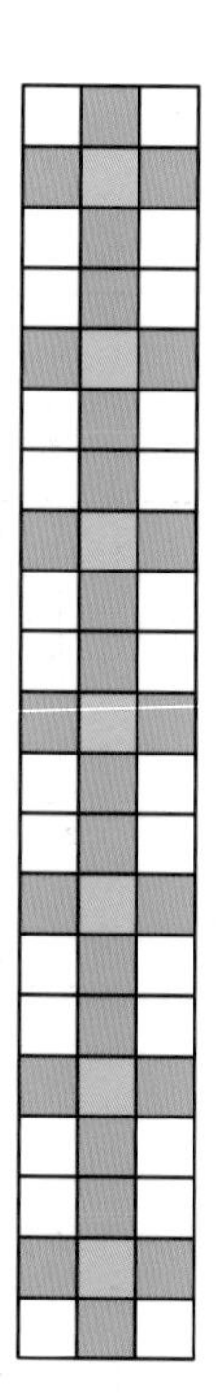

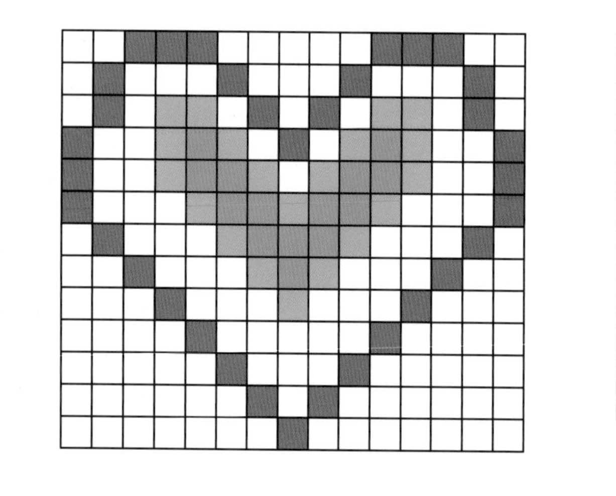

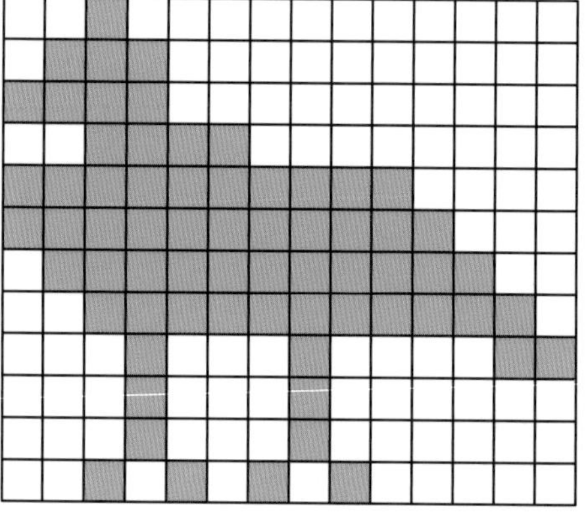

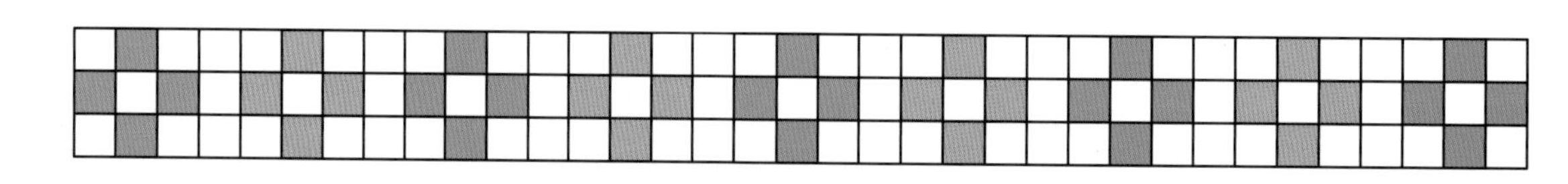

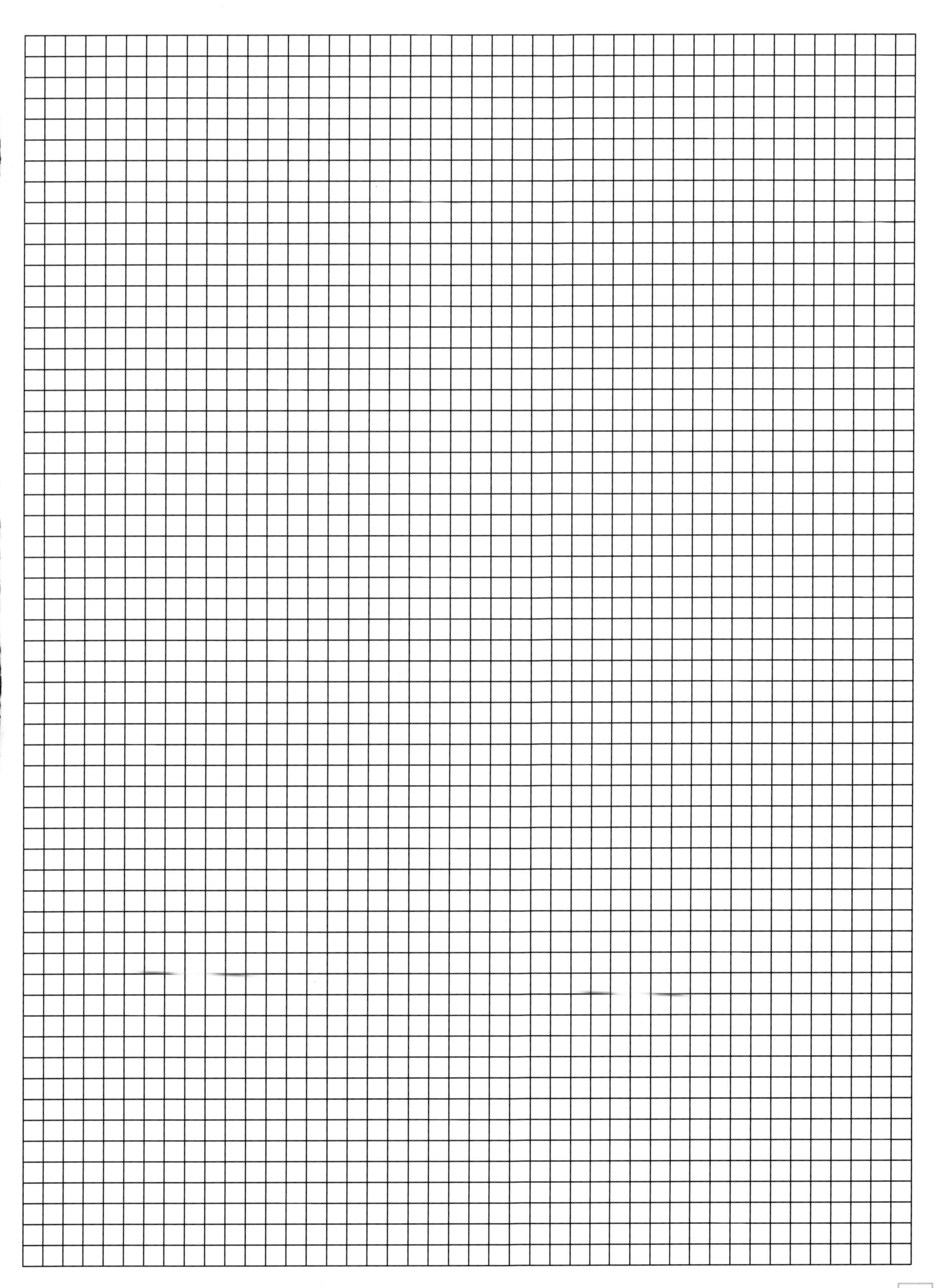

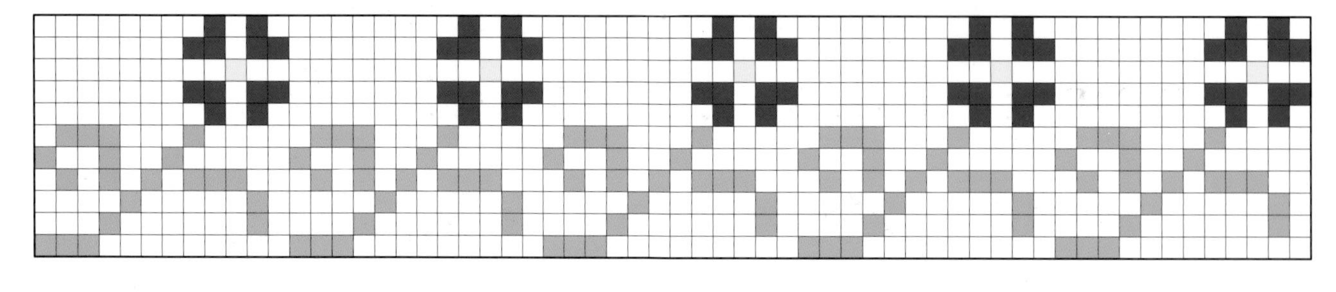

About the Author

Terry Martin, author of *Row by Row*, has been working with needle, thread, and cloth since she was thirteen. Her grandmother ("Gammy") taught her the finer points of needlework, and she has never looked back. For years Terry's true passion was cross-stitch, although she tried quilting in the 1970s (she still uses the resulting heavy, king-sized, denim quilt, backed by a percale sheet, for picnics). In the last five years, since discovering the rotary cutter, Terry has returned to quilting and has found it to be wonderfully rewarding. She now designs quilts, teaches quilting classes, and has a full-time job, supported in all by her loving and understanding family.